A Million Mosquito Bites

Notes from Honduras

H.E. CHRISTOFF

Produced by:

FriesenPress
Suite 300 – 852 Fort Street
Victoria, BC, Canada V8W 1H8

www.friesenpress.com

Distributed to the trade by The Ingram Book Company

Contents

With Much Gratitude

I want to thank RJ and CM for opening their home and hearts in friendship and understanding.

I want to thank my dear husband Peter for coming on this crazy adventure with me for over 25 years.

I want to thank my sister-in-law Cathy for many hours proofreading and offering me valuable feedback.

Love
Hilda
xoxo

Introduction

I am writing this book for the second time. I wrote the whole thing a few years ago when my husband said he wanted to read it and for some reason I couldn't find it anywhere on my computer. I wrote all those pages, spent months of my time and then I couldn't find it. Somehow it got deleted. Can you imagine?

Now to be fair, I think that when I originally created it I was looking at this story from a totally different perspective and not the way I see it today. I didn't think I would ever share it. I never thought anyone would find it interesting except my husband or my family.

I kept a journal when I was in Honduras, writing down anything silly, funny or strange that happened. It had no order or flow. It was just random thoughts and comments about what was going on that day. I thought if I documented it all, my husband Peter might find my perspective interesting compared to how he remembered it. I think this is a very different book from the one I previously wrote. Let's see how it turns out this time!

Germination: noun, plural: germinations

The stage in which a plant or fungus emerges from a seed or spore and begins growth. The most common example of germination is the sprouting of a seedling from a seed of an angiosperm or gymnosperm. In a more general sense, germination can imply anything expanding into greater being from a small existence or germ.

This is a story about sweating and itching. It is about food and cravings for food. It is about the power of gardening and discovery. It's about tenacity and finding a way to get what you need when it's not so easy. It's about overflowing abundance and tiny shards of joy in times of difficulty. It's about being uncomfortable and knowing who you are and who you are not. It's about the hard stuff and stupid stuff.

Glass .... it makes me think of glass. There are so many things made of glass, with glass, have glass in it, or on it. Is it shiny, is it etched, is it worn by sand at the beach, is it sharp, is it smoothed over by time? It has incredible strength or it can shatter into a thousand pieces. You can look through it, you can be protected by it, it can be a barrier, it can create fire, and it can help you see.

It's not what you look at in life, it's what you see! I can look at what you look at and see something completely different. This is how I saw it and what I interpreted from that view.

This is my story of 6 months in Honduras.

Looking back...

I think it started years ago with those damn calendars. My husband, Peter, bought calendars every year with the same thing on it... Beaches. They all looked like the same calendars to me and for years he assured me they were all different beaches, different palm trees, different tropical locations. Growing up in Canada he always wanted to live someplace tropical. If only we could quit our jobs and move someplace warm. We said it every winter and on every vacation. The thought of living someplace hot inspired great dreams.

One day the opportunity presented itself. Poof!

Right there, in front of us was a chance to live someplace hot, at the beach, doing something fun and different. It might be a chance to change our lives. It might be a chance to set ourselves up for a healthy retirement.

We held hands, closed our eyes and jumped! We said YES.

We would be moving to Honduras for three years. We would help with the building of a new housing project and be a part of something completely different.

The Adventure Begins...

It seemed as though the packing would simply never end. The amount of crap collected over thirteen years is really quite stupendous. I would clear out one room only to find more odds and ends in the next. How is it possible that this is unending in a 900 square foot house? Imagine if we actually had a normal sized house.

Peter is a saint. When I start wandering in circles not knowing what to do next, he calmly guides me to the next individual task at hand. Like a child he sat me down and told me exactly what to do. When the dogs had quite enough, he told me to leave, go for a walk, play in the yard. Without distractions he calmly and methodically did what was necessary to finish the preparations.

Finally, the last thing is packed away and the doors get locked on the 40 foot shipping container. We say goodbye to our home of 13 years, have one last pee and lock the doors.

I am scared and excited and nervous.

Our house in Ontario

The morning of the trip I am panicking, dreading our journey with two old dogs, set in their ways, pampered and accommodated their whole lives. They are two little mixed terriers named Molli and Lulu. I was anxious to make sure they did "their business" before we got in the car. We have practiced with the carriers for weeks leading up to the trip but nothing as long as the day ahead of us.

The dogs were surprisingly good in the car. They are settling down quite easily and even the airport was not so bad. I was grateful I bought the slightly bigger carriers. This was one time I said "screw you" to the precise dimensions that both American and Taca airlines had insisted the dogs be in. In the end none of them cared about the carriers which made me so happy we focused on comfort rather than the rules.

They were surprising well behaved in the airport. When one was having a hard time, the other was calm. I was so grateful for my little bottle of Bach Flowers Rescue Remedy, a natural flower essence to calm. I must confess I used it for myself as much as I did for them.

Our first leg was Toronto to Miami, a 2 ½ hour flight in duration plus the hanging around beforehand through security, etc. Nothing traumatic has happened and there were no problems. This might just turn out ok.

Walking out of the airport in Miami is like opening a door to a steam room. It is frigging hot and muggy here!

I was hoping to find some grass so Molli and Lulu would go pee. We went outside the terminal to the smoking area. The ground was green alright but, that was only from the green asphalt shingles covering the ground. No shit, there were shingles on the ground. The dogs had never pee'd on asphalt so convincing them to go was a bit of a challenge. Lulu was willing to go on the puppy training pads we had. Molli required grass and that was that. She decided she was holding it.

We head back into the airport for the next leg of our journey and we have finally managed to settle down the dogs again. There appears to be a small problem.... One of us is missing a ticket from San Pedro Sula to La Ceiba. Let's see if Roger can work his magic on the airline? We will be staying with Roger and Carly temporarily in Honduras and we are all traveling together. An hour later and many "not possibles", we have no additional flight and Roger is calling someone to come get us in San Pedro Sula. So now we will drive from San Pedro Sula to Trujillo. Great, after eleven hours of traveling we get to drive another five!

The praying begins..."Please dear God just let me get there so my dogs don't explode pee all over the plane."

Our flight from Miami to San Pedro Sula is in first class. We figured we needed the leg room with the dogs. It is a nice plane and everything appears great. The ride starts off ok. Lulu and Molli are not bothered by the takeoff and they seem to be settled.

The couple in front of us have a two year old boy with them and he decides he will scream at the top of his lungs every 20 seconds. He screams like those horns in a can at a baseball game. For the entire flight he screams. It is not a little raised voice, where a child sounds like they are fascinated by their own voice. No.... Marco makes an ear piercing scream every 20 seconds and his parents never tell him to stop! He NEVER stops, not even once. Everyone around us is pissed because little Marco is really enjoying listening to his own yelling and he is disturbing everyone in the front of the plane.

Molli starts to freak out in her carrier. Does she have to pee? I take her to the washroom and manage to put a pee pad on the floor while balancing on the toilet. I am hoping she will have room to go. She will not go. Nothing calms her. I go back to my seat and while hyperventilating, I then proceed to ask Peter every two minutes "are we there yet?"

More praying..."Oh God! Please let this flight be over. Make them land in a field preferably with lots of grass. Just get me off this fucking plane. If you could you make that child mute for the next 32 minutes that would be super. I am not asking for long term effects, just for the next 32 minutes and I will consider you a just and kind God". I am taking Rescue Remedy as much as I am feeding it to the dogs. Finally, the plane actually lands.

We arrive in San Pedro Sula and then we have to wait for the vet to show up. He will essentially take our money and say "yes stupid gringa your dogs are fine. You may enter". I beg them to let me take the dogs outside to the grass for a pee and a security guard escorts me through the gawking crowd and out to the grass. Man is it hot here! After 13 hours Molli FINALLY has a big, long, satisfying pee! I am so happy; you would have thought I was the one peeing.

Prayer answered. Thank you, God. They did not explode and I am on Terra Firma.

Everyone outside is looking and pointing at us because we just brought dogs on a plane and we have our dogs on a leash. What do you need a leash for? Plus they don't have any little dogs here. We are quite the spectacle. They stare and discuss. We are simply fascinating. I always wanted to be in the circus. Guess this is my chance and I didn't even have to grow a beard.

The vet finally comes, takes our money and they enter our details in the computer. When they ask how old my dogs are, the girl makes a double take when I say Molli is 15. She says "months?" I say "years" and their eyes open wide and they shake their heads. Dogs just don't live to 15 years here. Upon further thought maybe it is because they cannot believe we would pay all this money to bring over old dogs. Why spend money when you can go down any street and have one for free? They must think we are so stupid.

So… we meet Joe who is there to pick us up and we load up the Pathfinder. I am so excited that there is air conditioning in the truck. We sit in the back with our dogs happily beside us and they fall fast asleep for two and a half hours, dead exhausted. I am calm again, like I took a muscle relaxant calm. Imagine how good I will feel when I finally get a glass of wine in me?

We have decided we have to stop for dinner at Appleby`s. Fuck! I am in Central America with two dogs at 9 pm at night. (We got up at 4:30 am.) And now I have to go into a noisy restaurant sneaking my dogs in carriers so they don't die of heat in the truck.

We get seated in a booth at the back of the restaurant and there is a band playing right in front of our table. I am panicking and hoping we can hurry… Could there be any more trauma? Five minutes into sitting in the restaurant I feel the bags moving and jumping. They are both freaking out. I apologize and say I will wait in the car.

Let us pray again...."Please dear God, please, please let them miraculously have fast service for the only time ever in Honduras. Let no one get something they didn't order and may no one get any ideas of having a second drink or dessert. Thank you." I am so having a glass of wine when I get there.

When we finally arrive at the house it's late and it's quiet. I am so happy to see those front gates. My dogs can finally get out and walk around, have something to eat and relax in this new world. It's time for me to have that nice, big glass of wine.

I am grateful. I say my final prayer for the day. "Dear God, thank you for getting all of us here and not letting us die on a Honduran highway at night. Tomorrow will be a new day."

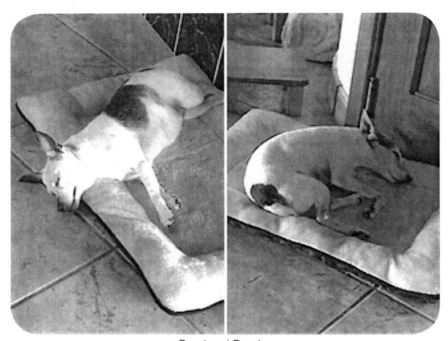

Dead and Deader

✳ July 8, 2008 - Day 1

I cried and cried and cried. Big, loud, wailing, sobbing, embarrassing noises are coming from me and I can't control myself. I am not even a crier; in fact I can't stand those women who cry at the drop of a hat for no reason. I am the person that looks at your 10 year old daughter who can't handle the excitement of her birthday wondering "what the hell is wrong with that kid?" Why is she crying when she is actually happy? I have a hard time with uncontrolled emotions and look at me. It's day one and I am a mess. What in hell was I thinking moving to Honduras in July? Just in case I didn't mention, it's bloody hot at the equator.

It's hot and humid. It's 85 degrees F or 30 degrees C with 80% humidity. It's hot as August in New Orleans hot. It's Cat on a Hot Tin Roof hot. It's Long Hot Summer hot. It's walk on the bloody sun hot. It never gives up. You dream of a cool breeze that never comes. I cannot believe people live here. I feel so Canadian.

I am not used to being this hot. The only places you can escape to is an air conditioned vehicle, which is the best or, our bedroom. We have a window air conditioner built into the wall. During the day the room is not much cooler maybe 25 – 28 degrees C. This is our own fault because we refuse to close the door completely in order for the dogs to come in and out.

We are staying with our friends Roger and Carly, in their home until we can build our own. We have been here three times before at various times of the year but, nothing can prepare you for the summer or for living in someone else's home even if it is a palatial 5000 square foot casa on the beach. I can barely think of anything except how hot I am and pray that 3 years comes soon. What will I be like on day two?

Peter is taking to this like a duck in water. He loves the sun and the water and is excited to start our new life. I knew he would like it better than I would. Tomorrow will be a better day.

Look at Peter all cool and comfortable

❋ July 9, 2008

I miss my old grocery stores. When we go into Trujillo, which is the closest town, there are a few grocery stores and a couple of fruit and vegetable stands we can shop at. If you go to the larger towns you can shop in bigger stores but, nothing like the North American grocery stores I am used to.

The first stop is the Supermarcado Popular. In this store you can get some frozen chicken (that is the only kind of chicken you can get in town), pop, beer, alcohol, toilet paper, Pringles or candy. It's a store that sells boxed, canned, preserved goods or cleaning products and other household necessities. The owner sells some perishables like milk and crema (which is like whipped cream and sour cream combined) and some sliced Bimbo bread (great name!). If you want fruit and vegetables you need to go to the stands near the market in the centre of town. I like the owner of the Supermarcado. She is always very nice. She thinks we are funny and laughs at the things we buy. She is helpful and happy to sell us anything we want.

When you go to the fruit and vegetable stalls you are immediately struck by the fact that everything looks so tired and small. It is partly because the market is out in the open with no spraying water, no ice or refrigeration. It is summer and it is so hot that things just get limp and tired very quickly. Our area is also pretty limited from an agricultural perspective. There are not many farmers near us growing produce for this little market. You need to take what you can get.

There are some large plantations that grow bananas for export and palms for palm oil production on the way to La Ceiba, a few hours out of town. Coffee and cocoa are also grown in the mountains. Honduras is rugged and mountainous and because it is a poor country most people in the remote towns are unaware of basic farming practices like how to enrich the soil in order to grow produce. Sadly, at the basic individual level most people only grow things that grow without effort like mango trees, some lime trees and coconut palms. Your average home does not have a vegetable plot to supply the home with fresh food and when times are hard, people revert to eating what is the cheapest and will sustain them, beans and rice.

When you do get the products that have been grown locally by individuals it is a very limited selection and poorly grown in less than ideal conditions. I can buy a few things consistently. I can buy white onions, some tomatoes, cucumbers, green peppers and iceberg lettuce. Sometimes you can get a decent watermelon. If you saw these vegetables in any city in North America they would have been the ones the grocer had picked to sell reduced or to throw away. I simply have to look at things from a different perspective; I need to see this all through a new set of eyes. I know I have brought with me at least $150 worth of vegetable and fruit seeds so that I don't have to live with my current options forever. I will grow the things I cannot buy and maybe I can share my seeds and gardening knowledge with others so that they may also benefit.

This is a part of the main street coming into Trujillo

✳ July 10, 2008

We go next door and say hello to Roger's neighbors. Karl and Judy are retired ex-pats from Canada who have lived here for many years. The cost of living is good. They get to live on the beach and their money buys them way more house than it does in Canada. They can afford to hire people to help them as they get older and this would simply not be possible on their pensions in Canada. There are several people from Canada and the US that have moved here for the same reasons. It's so much cheaper at every level.

The fact that the rum is dirt cheap helps too!

Karl and Judy have a lovely home that they share with their two Weimaraner dogs. They have done some really nice landscaping on their property. Judy is quite the gardener and has an impressive little production of palms going in one area. She has also taken cuttings and seeds from all over to create a lovely flowering garden. They even have a little vegetable patch at the back of their property that provides lots to eat. I will have to learn from their experiences and hopefully we can get a nice little production going here. I am hopeful that we can have enough produce to supply us and the families that are on the property. If I can help show them how to garden and we all work together like a co-op we can all learn and reap the edible rewards at harvest time. Karl and Judy tell me of all the challenges that have occurred to grow things by the ocean and things that need protection from the sun, from the wind or from the torrential rain when it falls. Then they tell me about the creatures like the large black and white, spiny tailed iguanas that run across the lawn. They will eat everything in your garden unless you protect your small plants with cages.

✳ July 11, 2008

I decide to start very small with two flower beds that are just outside the kitchen window. I have asked if we can transplant the bushes that are currently planted in them to grow a few herbs and vegetables. I will ask the watchmen in the next few days if they can remove the bushes and I will add some new soil and try to plant some seeds. It's all very exciting.

✳ July 12, 2008

We have come to Honduras to help our friends as well as to make a new life for ourselves. There is a plan to build the area with new homes and tourist attractions, restaurants, a park system, a working farm and a cruise ship terminal plus so many other projects. Roger has fantastic vision and a really exciting plan, along with the backing to make it happen. He has been working on this for several years and we are at the initial stages of building roads and the infrastructure to support the first housing subdivision. Once the roads are in we will oversee the building of the first 25 vacation homes. Most of the parcels of land are already sold and many people are excited and anxious to come, to be a part of the next Costa Rica. We are here to help in any way we can but, initially to oversee the construction of the roads and houses.

This is a tough environment for various reasons. There are cultural and language barriers, red tape and road blocks. Systems and people make progress very slow. Many have tried and given up but, I do believe if anyone from the outside can make this happen it is Roger. He is tenacious and committed and as persistent as a terrier. The main reason it will work is because he lives here and he truly loves it. He has made a home here for the past 15 years, and has already invested in this small community in many ways. He comes many times a year and brings lots of guests to experience the second home he wants others to enjoy and appreciate. I don't doubt for a second that the load will be heavy, the task list unending and that the challenges will be monumental at times. This is just the very beginning. Take a deep breath and start.

✳ July 13, 2008

I ask where I can buy top soil. They look at me strangely and say nowhere. I ask if there are any farm supply stores or a nursery where they might sell plants. They say no. I ask them how they plant things? How do they get good soil? They say you just add "caca de vaca" to your plants. Caca de vaca is cow shit.

The soil here is hard clay or just sand. There is nothing nice about it. It is crappy, depleted, dead DIRT and adding "caca de vaca" would be a start but, there has to be a way to make or find some good soil. Maybe I can take some of the fish manure from the river or dry some seaweed or start a compost heap to create my own fertilizer?

✳ July 14, 2008

Peter went into La Ceiba which is two hours away. If you can imagine there is actually an Ace Hardware store there. He found two tiny little bags of seed starter mix. The bags must have been in the store for years looking at the amount of dust on them. I think this is great, better than nothing or using the existing dirt, which is what I have had up to this point. Maybe I can start some seeds inside the house and once they have germinated I will plant them in my new kitchen garden bed. There has to be some nurseries in this country. Roger has hired a designer for the parks system they want to put in. Perhaps Henry the designer will know? I will ask next time I see him.

I find it so strange that there are no lemon trees here. There are lime trees but, they don't even know what a lemon is when I describe it. They call limes "limone" and when I ask for the yellow ones they say they don't like those. They like the limes and that is what they use. There are a few orange trees on Roger's property but, they are a type of wild orange that are full of seeds. They have been really sour every time I have ever been here before. I have heard they are sweet at the end of the summer so I am looking forward to trying them again when they are ripe. I have not seen any lemons or grapefruit on trees anywhere or in the markets but, I am told they do exist. I am finally in a place hot enough to grow lemons and grapefruits and I can't find any!

✳ July 15, 2008

Peter asks many people and eventually he finds someone who will sell us some decent dirt seeing as how we are stupid enough to pay for it. We can buy the dirt but, we have to bring our own bags or containers. So for a few lempiras (a few dollars) Peter comes home with 5 potato sacks and 1 rice sack full of dirt. I am so excited. I fill the top of the flower beds with some better dirt but wish I could have a hundred sacks. Oh well, small steps. I think I need to create my own production or this will never happen if I have to rely on a couple bags from time to time.

✳ July 16, 2008

You need to find a way to have a reserve of food. If you can store things in the freezer or pantry you don't have to go to town every day. I would like to eventually get a large freezer and get the pantry well stocked. I am not there yet but, I will. I would like to have enough food at all times so that if something happens you have at least a week's worth of food available at your fingertips.

✳ July 17, 2008

Today I went into the big town of La Ceiba. I found much more produce available at the big grocery store although it's still pretty sad looking. I was able to find some imported apples from Chile and Barilla pasta which I cannot buy in Trujillo. Last Friday I was craving pasta and there was none available in town so I decided to make my own. Normally this is not a big deal. I am a competent home cook and have made pasta before however, this time I didn't have my KitchenAid mixer with the pasta attachment. I had to do it all by hand. I made the dough with no problems and then I rolled it out with a bottle because like my mixer my rolling pin is packed in my shipping container. I imagine that they are all safely making their voyage over the ocean at this very moment. The finished product turned out just fantastic. It was very exciting. I had a can of tomatoes so I made some sauce and we had a lovely Italian dinner. In reality I don't know if it really was that good or was it simply because we hadn't had it in a while that we just thought it was so awesome? Just like when you are craving a bag of chips and you see someone else with some, they give you one and you think "why are these chips so damn good? How come chips don't taste this good when I buy them?" Who knows? What I do know is that I need to grow me some basil!

✳ July 18, 2008

Sifting: verb
1. *To put a fine, loose or powdery substance through a sieve to remove lumps or large particles.*
2. *To examine something thoroughly so as to isolate that which is most important or useful.*

Today I decided to see if the oven works. The range is gorgeous. It's a brand new KitchenAid gas range however; there is no gas connection to the house. The stove top has been converted to propane and for some reason it never gets hot enough. The oven is electric so I know it will be ok. I have lots of ripe bananas and have decided to try to make a banana cake. I have gone on the web to find a recipe which I need to modify with the ingredients I can get here to see if it will work. The bananas have to be kept in the fridge because if you left anything with sugar in it on the counter within minutes it will be covered in these teeny tiny micro-ants. The recipe calls for baking soda and they do not sell baking soda in Trujillo, so I do a search on the web to see if I can substitute baking powder. They say you can however, you need to double or triple the amount used and then omit any salt in the recipe. This recipe has crème fraiche as an ingredient which I absolutely cannot get here but, I can buy crema which might work in future. I do have some coconut milk on hand so I will use that. It doesn't have the acid like the crème fraiche but, I will give it a try. I bake the cake and it turns out fantastic! I love it when it works out. The oven works fine, however it heats up the kitchen by at least 20 degrees. Just what we don't need is a hotter kitchen.

Once the cake is done you can cool it on the top of the stove which is still hot however, you must eat the entire cake before the stove cools down or the micro-ants will come. I wonder if I should tell people to eat the entire cake before it cools off? We eat as much of the cake as we can and either I have to put the rest in the fridge which is not ideal because the fridge is a moist environment, or option two is to cut up the rest and give it to Judy and Karl to enjoy while it's still at its prime. I choose to give it away. Baking is for sharing anyways.

Banana Walnut Coconut Cake

3 ¼ cups flour (white or corn are the only kinds of flour available here)

3.5 tsp baking powder

½ tsp. ground cinnamon

4 eggs – room temperature

2 1/3 cups sugar

1 cup olive oil or vegetable oil

3 cups mashed ripe bananas

¼ cup coconut milk (canned) or crème fraiche or crema

2 tsp. rum (they don't sell vanilla here)

1 cup walnuts

1/3 cup shredded coconut

- Heat oven to 350 degrees F. You can make this in 2 loaf pans or I used one large glass Pyrex dish. Prepare pan(s) by buttering and flouring pan(s). Tap pan(s) to make sure all excess flour is discarded.

- Sift all dry ingredients together flour, baking powder, cinnamon into a bowl or on a piece of wax paper.

- In a large bowl with a mixer, or by hand, beat eggs and sugar at medium speed until thick and pale. This may take a few minutes. Add oil and mix 2 more minutes. Add mashed bananas, coconut milk and rum.

- Mix in dry ingredients by hand until just incorporated. Finally add walnuts and coconut.

- Pour into prepared pan(s). Bake 1 to 1 ½ hours. The cake is done when a toothpick inserted into the centre comes out clean.

- Cool 10 minutes in pan(s) then turn onto a cooling a rack (turn cake right side up) or just slice out of the Pyrex dish.

- You can top with powdered sugar, a chocolate glaze, a coconut glaze or nothing at all! It's all delicious and very moist.

- This cake can also be wrapped in plastic wrap and frozen.

✳ July 19, 2008

Craving: noun

An intense desire for something

Synonyms: longing, desire, lust, thirst, hunger, eagerness

I am frustrated by the simple things I cannot get in Trujillo that you would never think of until you need to cook or bake something you are used to. They do not sell whipping cream or baking soda. You cannot buy unsalted butter (only salted). They sell no yogurt at all. A red, yellow or orange pepper is unheard of. There are no greens like spinach or Swiss chard. No herbs like cilantro, parsley or basil. You can get culantro which has a similar taste to cilantro and in fact they call it cilantro. No lemons, oranges or grapefruits.

Why do I want to eat everything I can't have? Isn't it always the way?

✳ July 20, 2008

Dulce de Leche–

is the most common name for milk caramel in Spanish. It is popular in Latin America. It is used to sweeten candies, cookies or ice creams and can be used as a spread. It is made from boiling or baking sweetened condensed milk in the unopened can in a water bath for 3-4 hours until it turns into a thick caramel like product.

Today is Peter's birthday and Marco made a point yesterday of insisting that he would be coming over to give Peter a birthday cake. Marco was hired to be Peter's translator and help him manage the daily things he needs to accomplish during the initial phase of the project. Marco has told me at least four times to expect him today and he has secretly told me his mother has prepared a beautiful birthday cake for Peter.

Marco is recently divorced and much to his embarrassment is living with his mother again. First thing in the day we get a call from Marco reminding us again to expect him. A few hours later we get a call to tell us he is still trying to find someone to drive him to the house as we are about a 15 minute drive from where he lives. Finally Marco arrives in someone's car with a large cake in hand. It is a white cake thickly covered in Dulce de Leche. Most homes do not have refrigeration and so a Dulce de Leche cake makes sense here. There is no such thing as whipping cream available in our little town and the only butter you can buy is heavily salted so butter cream frosting like most cakes are made with in North America is not a good option. Dulce de Leche is made from condensed milk and will not melt like some of the other choices made with fresh dairy. Marco is so proud to present us with the cake and wishes Peter the very best for his birthday. I cut us a few slices and make some fresh coffee.

We are used to the taste of a cake with a butter cream frosting or a sweet chocolate icing. This cake is very heavy and the icing is very, very sweet. I don't like it at all and find it almost sickeningly, cloyingly sweet and thick like caramel. I can tell that Peter doesn't either but, he is too polite to say anything. I know this because of his facial expressions as well as the fact I know Peter only likes two things for dessert: chocolate chip cookies or any kind of chocolate cake. He doesn't want to hurt Marco so he graciously eats every single bite. I can't do the same and pretend my slice is too big and that I will save it for later.

We chat for a while over our coffees and learn how Marco dreams of becoming a minister and how he fears this will never be possible since he is divorced. The divorce is a big disappointment for him and after all this time it is still a huge shock. He just can't understand what happened and why his wife would leave. I have a few ideas but, not a good topic of conversation on this fine day.

Finally, Marco decides he has had enough and asks if Peter can drive him home. Peter is dying to enjoy his birthday with just the two of us and now he has to drive the guy home. He obviously spent all his favours getting a ride out here and the only other option is to walk back. Peter obligingly gets in the truck and takes him home. When Peter gets back we enjoy a nice lunch of some grilled chicken and Peter gets to go for a swim in the pool. It feels really nice to be just enjoying the hot day in the cool pool.

You just never know what you will come across on the road to Trujillo

✳ July 22, 2008

Everyone who comes to the house is utterly fascinated by how old my dogs Molli and Lulu are. It is a recurring conversation and people continue to be amazed. They have never seen dogs that are as old as mine in their lives. They see that the dogs are females but they don't understand why they haven't had any puppies. Every female dog they have seen has nipples that clearly indicate they have nursed pups. Why don't my dogs look like that? We tell them they are fixed, that the dogs had surgery to prevent them from having puppies. They look at us and shake their heads in disbelief. Most people here cannot even imagine paying money to buy dog food much less paying a vet to spay or neuter is simply unimaginable. In fact there is not even a vet in town. You would have to go to Tacoa or La Ceiba if you wanted to see one and even there the vet only exists because of the ex-pats who use it. Your average Honduran in this area would never use the services of a vet in their lives for a pet dog.

✳ July 23, 2008

People are always coming to the house for meetings or to do some kind of work around the property. We have put up wooden baby gates on several of the doors so that the dogs will stay in but, the doors must remain wide open or you would die from the heat. When people come to the door, they always spend a few minutes staring and looking at the engineering involved in the construction of the gate. We often find people standing there looking at them from every angle before they come in. They ask what they are for and when we tell them to keep the dogs in they always look at us and wonder why. Most could not even imagine a baby gate for a baby. In all homes, both babies and dogs simply spill out on the road. Either they learn quickly to get out of the way of cars or else they have an older brother or sister who is designated guardian to make sure they are not hit on daily basis... the children that is. No one does this for the dogs. They just better figure it out or die young. Visitors to the house are convinced we are totally nuts.

✳ July 24, 2008

Today I am missing my clothes dryer. Sheets are wonderful when you dry them out in the sun on a clothes line but, towels... not so much. This reminds me of my childhood because we never had a dryer either. We always had a ringer washer even after the new washers came out. My mother went out of her way to find the old fashioned ringer washer when her old machine died. This was the machine she knew and the only kind she wanted. There was never even a thought of buying a dryer. In the summer you hung out the wash in the backyard and in the winter you hung it up in the basement. The towels were always like cardboard, never soft and fluffy, smelling wonderful right out of the dryer. I should be grateful that we have a washing machine inside of the house; if you have a washing machine here it is almost always outside. I guess they want the machine outside close to the clothes line. Because it is so humid here almost everything will get rusty or mouldy sooner than any other place on earth. You drive by any nicer home and you always see the washing machines outside and they are usually all rusty.

I sometimes feel like I am in an episode of Sanford and Son.

✳ July 25, 2008

Damn it is hot here! I am obsessing about my discomfort again. It's all consuming, I am hot and sticky and I don't know how to cool off. How can I find a way to get more comfortable? I don't mind sweating if I am doing a workout or if I am in a sauna however, just pouring sweat all day long is gross. Even the people who are not "sweaters" would sweat in Honduras in July.

✳ July 26, 2008

We went into La Ceiba to go to the bank today. Hilarious! First, when you get to the Banco you are greeted at the door by a security guard with a rifle and a metal detector wand. You must turn off your cell phone at the door. Don't ask me why. You must make sure you leave your gun or your machete in the car and men are required to "spread 'em" so that the guards can check for weapons. They do not do this on women for some reason. I guess they have decided only the men could do anything bad. Hmmm? Note to self: if I am ever planning a bank heist, do it with broads!

You are then allowed to go through the first set of doors but then you are required to wait in this air lock until the first set of doors is locked behind you and only then will the second set of doors be opened by the next guard. He then unlatches the little garden latch that is on the second set of doors. I guess they feel they have guns so they don't really need the high tech doors just yet. Then you go to a huge waiting area and sit with at least 30 other people who are also waiting. In this country you will learn patience.

Within a few minutes we are somehow bumped and we get called to come to the teller window. We discover that the one woman who speaks English is available to help us. I wonder why there are chairs in front of the tellers? I have come in to be added to an existing bank account that my husband has already set up and they need to see my documents, so this should probably not take very much time.

I very quickly understand what the chairs are for when she proceeds to fill out every detail on paper application forms and then once this is all done she must then enter it all again into the computer. How ridiculous is this? It takes two hours to be added to an existing account. She asks some bizarre questions which have already been answered on the application like: "how many children do you have?" She is asking this for a bank account? Ok... none. She looks at me suspiciously... really none, at your age? Then she asks what my education level is. To be added to a bank account...really? While she is doing all of this, there is a supervisor behind her and she has to get each item approved before she is able to enter it into the computer. I thought banks in Canada were ridiculous in some of their archaic processes and procedures but, they have nothing on the banks here. I am sitting in my chair with my mouth open for most of this... I feel like I am in the twilight zone. As I leave the bank I figure they must think every gringo here must be a drug dealer. Truly bizarre!

We decide since we are here to go across the parking lot to the Carrion department store. I am hoping to buy several things on my list that I cannot buy in Trujillo. You always have a list that you carry everywhere. It may take weeks or even months to finally get everything checked off. When we walk in I am in a rush and want to quickly get what I need and go. I am so impatient after being in that bank for so long.

Immediately we are approached by several people asking us if they can help. I look at the first item on my list and say "yes, I need hangers". They walk around in circles and have no idea where they are. I ask for the next thing on the list and it is the same. They have so many people working there and no one knows where anything is. Is this because I am asking for things they would personally never use in their lives or just because no one knows where anything is? This is so painful. I just lose patience and go off on my own and find everything I need based on where they would logically be in any department store. They think there is something wrong because I am walking so fast and in a hurry. No one is in a hurry here, ever! At this point I don't give a shit. I need to hurry and get out of here so I can go to the grocery store and then get back in the car and go home before it gets dark, which is at 6 pm.

You never want to drive on the roads after dark if you don't have to because it's dangerous. Strange things occur on the roads after dark and there *ain't* no street lights so it is pitch black for most of the trip. One person drives like a bat out of hell. The next car drives at 20 km per hour and has no lights on their car. There are pot holes half the size of your car and if you can't see them then you will just fall in. There are cows that sleep on the side of the road or people just hanging out on the road. Dogs and horses are everywhere. If you don't have to drive at night you don't. With a truck load of stuff we finally leave and make it home before dark. It took almost a whole day to go to the bank, the department store and the grocery store. Imagine it. No, really imagine it.

✳ July 29, 2008

I have a cold today and I feel like crap. I have a really bad sore throat. It is 30 degrees C and I get to drink hot tea which totally holds no appeal for me. I guess I will find out whether drinking hot liquids will actually cool down the body. I could never understand why so many people eat hot soup here when it's so damn hot. Guess I will try it.

After testing this theory, I have decided it doesn't work and I am still hot.

❋ July 30, 2008

Peter went to the Nissan dealership in La Ceiba today. He wants to buy a truck so he doesn't have to keep using Roger's. Peter needs a vehicle that he can fit in. He is 6 foot 5 and this is always a problem. He has decided he likes the Nissan Navara. Now the challenge is how we can arrange payment. Wiring large amounts of money is difficult around here. I suspect it's because of the problem with drugs but, I am guessing. Peter even asks if he can pay for the truck on his Visa card to see if this makes it easier. That sounds so strange to me but, he thinks why not if it is easier plus we would get the reward points. In the end they will not allow the sale on Visa and we do wire the money from Canada. Nice try big guy.

❋ August 1, 2008

Roger says "everything is easy in Honduras. It's just that it's all uphill." STRAIGHT UP! I would have to agree with that statement. Everything takes longer and everything is difficult. We went to the Carrion Department store in La Ceiba today to buy three televisions. We were buying them for Roger. He was putting them in the houses of the watchmen. There are three watchmen and they each have their own house on the property. They have been helping out in extra ways lately as there has been so much additional activity going on, so the televisions are a reward for all their hard work. This will be a huge luxury for them and I think they will be very happy. We go to the department store and pick out three televisions. We go to the cash register to pay and their computer system will not accommodate this purchase. We don't know if it is the amount of the purchase or volume of television sets? They get the manager and fifteen minutes later they still they do not know how to ring in the sale. We wait and wait. This is a large two storey department store; it looks like any normal modern department store that could be in any large city. They cannot figure out how to ring in three televisions. In the end they have to ring in each television individually. I shake my head and wonder what would happen if you bought 6 pairs of socks or 10 shirts? I actually want to try it just to mess with them however, it is mean and I don't have the patience so I just keep my evil little game to myself.

We put up the bug net on our bed last night. I think this was the first morning I didn't wake up with more mosquito bites than I had the night before. I am ecstatic! I have so many bites I am convinced I must already have malaria. My legs look like I have chicken pox. The mosquitoes here are not like in Canada. In Canada they are much bigger and you can usually hear them coming, so at least you have a fighting chance. In Honduras, the mosquitoes are more like no-see-'ems. You look down at your leg and notice it's completely bitten. I have to wear "Off" (Deet bug spray) all the time which totally freaks me out. It's sticky and I think "OMG I am spraying shit on my skin that could kill me". I am spraying poison on me all day on my largest organ. I have bought every alternative natural spray, shampoo, soap, cream and oil from Canada and nothing works. Even with the Off spray, I am still attractive to the mosquitoes.

Peter is dealing with the bite issue much better than I am and has many fewer bites than I do. Bastard! Maybe he is just not that tasty to them or maybe it's because he wears jeans, socks and boots all the time. For me, to even look at him makes me sweat! I would faint if I wore that. I wear a tank top, shorts and sandals and a bandana to try to catch most of the sweat that just rolls off me all day. If I wore pants I would instantly get a heat rash all over my legs. Hell, even wearing shorts, I get a heat rash at my knees and ankles. I am a mess. Oh, did I mention that these mosquito bites are ten times itchier than the ones you get in Canada? A bite can be itchy for a week and if you scratch a bite, it turns into a blister which disgustingly weeps and dries all crusty. I am an itchy, weeping, crusty, red, sweaty, horrible mess.

This is me fresh out of the shower

This is me fresh out of the shower so I am not sweating while I get my picture taken. Once the picture is taken I am pretty sure my top lip broke out in beads of sweat and I had to put down Lulu because she was generating too much heat.

✳ August 3, 2008

A bird flew into the house today. It was a beautiful baby kingfisher. The interior of the house is being painted and one of the painters helped me to catch the bird. When the bird got tired, the painter managed to throw a tea towel over him and was able to gently pick him up and put him outside. It was a moment of beauty to see a baby kingfisher up close and a moment of joy to see him fly away. There are few moments when I feel this sense of pure wonder here. That makes me sad. I need to find more moments like this. It was a really nice feeling just like being in love. I want to capture more moments that feel like that.

✳ August 4, 2008

Lulu went on an adventure today.

Peter went next door to Karl and Judy's place. We have baby gates that are put up on some doors and we have just barricaded the other doors with the cushions from the lounge chairs. Mostly the barricades are to protect Molli who would just fall down the stairs as her eye sight is not very good in her old age. There are a lot of doors in this big house. Lulu is pretty smart and knows how to hop over the gate or push her way through the cushions. I am constantly watching to make sure she is near me because there are so many cars that just come and go around here and most people would have no clue to watch for her. She is not like the normal dogs around here that have learned from just a few days old to get the hell out of the way or get squished. Lulu is a little princess and I can't trust she would be smart enough to get out of the way of danger.

There are many cars and no real fences as I know them except for barbed wire fencing that separates the neighbor's property and the beach etc. I am always cautious and aware of Lulu so she doesn't get into trouble. Normally she is my shadow and is always attached to me or at least in my view. She does adore Peter and likes to hang out near him so while I was cooking I took my eyes off of her for a few minutes and she snuck through the cushion barrier at the pool doors. She sniffs around and obviously finds the trail to where Peter has gone. She sniffs her way to the gate that separates Roger's property from Judy and Karl's. Now you need to picture a wooden gate however, the fence is four rows of barbed wire on posts all the way to the beach. Lulu decides this won't stop her and decides to just jump through the rows of barbed wire and go find Peter. She gets to Judy's house and waits at the bottom of their stairs. Judy happens to look down and see Lulu sitting there. She tells Peter and he quickly tries to go out to grab her before Judy's dogs discover the intruder. The dogs leap up as he moves and in a flash start to chase her. This is the first time Lulu has been around so many other dogs. She takes off like the wind and hops through the fence again, runs straight into the house and right to me in the kitchen. Mommy!

I can only wonder what has happened when Peter runs in breathless to tell me the story. We pick her up and notice a few cuts on her belly from the barbed wire but, other than that she is scared but fine. I am convinced she is part Italian greyhound and I am sure the speed part of her breed was to her advantage on this particular adventure. I am happy Molli is blissfully unaware and quite content wandering in the big house.

✳ August 5, 2008

I need to be more diligent with that dog. Lulu tried to follow Peter again today. He left in the truck and she decided she wanted to go with him. She just busted through a barrier when I wasn't watching and decided to follow him. There is a very long driveway that leads up to the front gate. She walked all the way up the driveway and almost got to the gate when the watchman at the front noticed her.

The one watchman called the other watchman on the radio to say that the princess was out. Since they have never seen her alone they figured something wasn't right. Manuel managed to chase Lulu all the way back to the house. This was in the middle of the day when it was very hot and she ran inside all scared and overheated. She also may have felt lost because this is a large property and she didn't know her way back. Manuel ran into the house after her and explained what happened to me in Spanish (which I figured out, understanding every other word along with hand gestures). I was so grateful she was ok. Lulu drank water for about two minutes and never left my side for the rest of the day.

Confidence and separation anxiety are a delicate balance in her little mind. If she had her way she would go with Peter in the truck on all his excursions. It's so funny that she loves the truck here since she rarely went for drives at all when we were in Canada.

I love this picture of Lulu – all tough looking – on the long driveway

✳ August 6, 2008

The banks are always a challenge here. Peter wanted to buy the Nissan truck he was looking at. For some reason the bank in Canada didn't transfer the money to the dealership, they wired the money to our account and now it is a huge ordeal to move the money to Nissan. It seems to be a big deal to have large sums of money deposited in your account here. The bank will not release or transfer the money unless we can prove we have a bill of sale for the truck. I think they assume anyone with money doing any transferring is laundering money. In the end it all worked out fine but, once again daily business is anything but normal or easy.

✳ August 7, 2008

I watched Manuelito playing today. Manuelito is the little son of Manuel... Makes sense to me. He is one of five children. He is 2 years old and has a younger baby brother. His father, one of the watchmen was working nearby and I couldn't take my eyes off Manuelito playing on the steps to the main house. He was playing with three bottle caps he found in the dirt. His father was digging up some bushes from the side of the house to move to a new bed around the driveway. Manuelito was perfectly content and happy to play with those bottle caps and never made a peep of discomfort. He drove them in the dirt like any child playing with toy cars. It was heart warming to watch his pleasant disposition and happy nature playing with something as simple as bottle caps.

When his father had gathered some palm fronds that needed to be taken over to the fire pit, he loaded the wheel barrow and simply plopped little Manuelito right on top of the pile. He has these old, wise eyes for such a young boy. He walks around barefoot in his shirt and underpants. I can't walk on the grass or on the driveway without shoes on and he manages perfectly fine with his tiny, little feet. He makes me smile because is so unaware of how cute he is. He is confident and curious but, also shy and sweet.

He looks like a big man in a little boy package.

Manuelito getting a ride in a wheel barrow

✳ August 8, 2008

There are four dogs that belong to Gilberto, Robelio and Manuel, the watchmen. Manuel has a dog named Solita (Little Sun), because she is blond, and another dog named Wobey (pronounced Whoa-Bee), a young black and tanned dog. Then there is Tigra (pronounced TEE-Gra) because she is striped like a tiger. Finally there is Cheezpa. I don't have a clue what his name means.

This is Solita

This is Solita. She is quite lovely. Today she let me pet her for the first time. I held her head in my hands and she let me scratch her ears. She is gentle and sweet and she almost fell asleep in my hands. I am sure she is not used to being the focus of attention like this very often. She is well treated by her owner and she exhibits signs of being a happy adjusted dog. She happily plays with her owners and the other dogs on the property.

She is lucky to have good owners but, make no mistake she is a dog with a job to help protect and watch the property and not a pet. Wobey is a boisterous young male. He always sneaks up on me and nips at my fingers but, is way too afraid to let me pet him. Tigra and Cheezpa are both shy and will not let me come near them.

✳ August 9, 2008

I have started to keep any leftover meat we have from our meals to give to Manuel for his dogs. I cannot imagine throwing it away when they need it. I never feed the dogs myself because I don't want them to associate me with food and come begging or decide they are brave enough to walk into the main house which would cause problems in the long run. So I happily give any food to Manuel and let him feed them.

Manuel's daughters are very cute. Whenever we see them they wave at me and then giggle to each other. Maria is the younger one and I can tell she is a little monkey and quite a handful. She is feisty and playful while her sister fits the oldest child role. You can tell she is responsible and already the biggest support for their mother.

✳ August 10, 2008

We ran out of propane today which means I can't use the stove. When you run out of propane you need to get someone to take the large tank to town. And of course they don't have any propane in Trujillo so the shop takes it to the next large town to have it filled. It gets returned to the house a few days later. I decide to make pizza tonight for dinner since I can use the grill to barbeque the chicken and I can still use the oven to bake since it is electric. I love a gas stove and it is normally better than electric but, not here. When I have my own house I am not doing this propane bullshit. I am getting electric because no one has to get the propane refilled and it will heat up properly as long as you have power. Electricity, now that is a whole other conversation.

The pizza turned out fantastic. I grilled the chicken, made the dough, put on barbeque sauce and sprinkled mozzarella cheese that was brought over from Canada. Whenever people travel here from Canada they always bring mozzarella or aged cheddar cheese with them. You just can't find good cheese here even in the larger grocery stores. I also found some large pizza pans in the kitchen that worked perfectly. You know, I should learn how to make my own cheese. Mozzarella is one of the easier cheeses to start with. Becoming a proficient cheese maker might be a very useful skill to have here.

✳ August 11, 2008

Lulu had a nice walk this morning on the beach. We have to go out very early before it gets too hot. Lulu is so funny to watch because she is still getting used to walking on sand. She is even letting her feet get wet when the sand is hot which is remarkable since she normally doesn't like getting her feet wet at all. It's so cute to watch her discovering this new place. Molli is older and couldn't stand the long walk and the heat so she happily stays inside walking around for most of the day and sleeping the rest. I am so glad they are with me.

I went out to the huge mango tree that is by the front door. I picked up six mangos from the ground. The tree is amazing. It is literally dripping with fruit from its higher limbs. If you stand under the tree for longer than a minute you hear the crack of mangos dropping. I washed them and put them in the fridge. I love them when they are icy cold. I can still recall the first time I tried mangos with my friends Lourdes and Jose back in Toronto. In their high park apartment I distinctly remember the way Jose peeled and sliced the cold fruit and served it as a cool summer treat. One taste and I was hooked.

There is always a steady stream of people walking over to the tree and they all use their shirts like a sling to carry away as many mangos as they can manage. The watchmen and their children come to collect mangos at least twice a day. Sometimes they bring big bowls but most times they also just use their shirts. When they eat them, they simply rip off the outer skin with their teeth and eat the soft juicy flesh. When they are finished they throw away the pit and grab another. That's how everyone eats them here. Here I am with my chilled mangos, peeling away the skin with a knife and slicing the flesh into neat strips. I am such a gringa.

You can eat as many mangos as you like! Go on have one!

✳ August 12, 2008

I can't understand why people from North America move here. Why do they come to this little, remote town? How do they wind up here? It is challenging to start a business if you are a foreigner. There have been some people who have successfully set up restaurants or hotels because they would be bringing tourists from where they come from or they could attract tourists on the web. Tourism is low in this remote area and business success is difficult if you are not a local. Maybe it's as simple as wanting to live in a place that is always warm. I can relate to that one. It explains why there are Canadians here. But why do the Americans live here? They have warmth in their own country. Is it the desire to live someplace warm and also cheap? I understand why you would want to live here if you were retired. If you don't have to work you can live very modestly. You can afford to hire people to help you do the things you progressively can no longer do and the warm weather and water is wonderful.

I am here to help with this project. I am here to make some money and hopefully to set ourselves up for a comfortable retirement. I can't imagine wanting to stay here for the rest of my days.

I hope it will get better, that I will like it more, maybe that I will fit in. For now, sadly I just don't see it.

✳ August 13, 2008

I am washing the tile floors in the corners of all the rooms today which are always thick with dirt. They are dirty because the woman who cleans uses a mop and just skims over the corners. They have built up with dirt over time and I hate looking at them. I have decided to take a bucket of water and an S.O.S. pad and get down on my knees and clean them. Within two minutes I am pouring water; it is rolling down my forehead and into my eyes. I have to stop what I am doing and put on my bandana so I can see. If I do anything remotely physical here I sweat. Cleaning corners in rooms is like a total workout at the gym. Ok... so this is a pro and a con of living here. At home I would have to be in a sauna or steam room or workout until I drop to sweat like this. Hmmm... A sauna sounds nice right now because it's a dry heat! Isn't that what they say about the desert? "Yeah it's a dry heat".

✳ August 14, 2008

Knead: verb
To mix and work into a uniform mass. To mix or shape by folding, pressing and stretching with the hands. To squeeze, press or roll with the hands, as in massaging

We went to Rogues Galleria today for lunch. I love going there. It is my favorite restaurant. It is a 10 minute drive to the beach road in town where it is located. We were the only two people there because we arrived early. We ordered two cold cervezas. Peter had a Corona and I had a Dominican Port Royal. As we were enjoying the view of the beach and the taste of our cold beer, an older woman walks into the restaurant from the beach. She has a rolled up towel placed on her head like a crown and on top of the towel is a plastic dish that is full of bread. She walks with the bread perfectly balanced on her head. She calls out "Pan de Coco! Pan de Coco!" Sometimes we buy her coconut bread but, it is as if she has some kind of radar. I think she has come in every time I have ever been there. Peter thinks she is from Santa Fe which is another town close by. She walks up along the beach and sells her bread and rolls every day.

We get our food. Lucita, the restaurant owner, is a great cook. For such a small restaurant she and her staff make the best food and this is my favorite place. I really like to be here. I get some battered fish chunks and fries and Peter has the chicken fajitas. Peter eats his fajitas with way too much salsa picante (hot sauce). He starts to sweat under his eyes and decides next time maybe he should put on just a little less.

We eat and watch a group of boys playing American football on the beach. They play in the deep sand along the water's edge. There are no time outs and out of bounds is when the ball ends up in the ocean. There is a big kid on one team that continuously ploughs through the little kids to score a touchdown. There is a little kid that is the quarterback and he is clearly the bossy, smart kid who owns the ball. I don't know how they pick teams but, you don't want to be on the opposite team from the one the big kid is on. We have affectionately dubbed the big kid "Baby Huey". The side that he is not on never gets possession of the ball and they all get crushed by him. It is totally hilarious to watch and they are obviously having a great time. We hoot and cheer and they are only too happy to entertain us. They wave and laugh while we pretend this game is on TV and provide the commentary from the bar. It is a nice lunch with good entertainment on a beautiful day.

✳ August 15, 2008

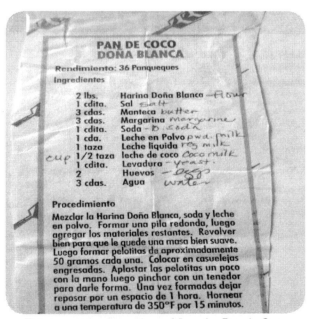

This is a recipe on my bag of flour for Pan de Coco

This is a recipe on my bag of flour for Pan de Coco but I don't know what kind of measurements they are or what the instructions are so, I decide to try to make my own recipe. I made the dough into small rolls and they turned out pretty darn good.

Pan De Coco

You will need:

½ cup warm water

2 tbsp. sugar

1 tbsp. dry yeast

½ cup shredded coconut

1 cup coconut milk

2 tbsp. melted butter

3 cups flour

1 tsp. salt

- Step 1: In a small bowl add warm water, sugar and yeast. Stir and leave 5 minutes to get foamy.

- Step 2: In another small bowl add shredded coconut, coconut milk and melted butter.

- Step 3: In a large bowl add dry ingredients: flour and salt.

- Step 4: Add the yeast mix to the coconut milk and stir. Add the wet ingredients to the dry and mix until it becomes too difficult to continue mixing in the bowl. Pour contents on to counter. Knead with your hands for 7-8 minutes until it is no longer sticky and forms a nice smooth dough.

- Step 5: Put dough in an oiled bowl and cover with plastic wrap. Let rise until it doubles in size. 1-2 hours. It is more important that the dough doubles in size even if it takes longer in terms of time.

- Step 6: Punch down dough and divide evenly into pieces. Form into smooth buns. Place on an oiled baking tray and let rise until doubled again in size. 45 minutes to 1 hour.

- Step 7: Brush with egg wash. Bake in a 350 degree F oven on middle rack for 20- 25 minutes or until golden brown.

✳ August 16, 2008

The watchman's younger daughter Maria came over to me today and told me how young all her dogs are and how Solita is the mother of Wobey and Tigra. She smiles at me and then just walks away. She is pretty cute. I pick up my dogs and kiss them both and tell them they are so lucky they live with me! If I was re-incarnated as a dog I would want to live with someone like me too. This is a funny place!

✳ August 17, 2008

We were in town today and on the drive back to the house we came through Cristales which is the Garifuna part of town. Garifuna is a term for the Afro-Caribbean people that live here. You always drive slowly through town because you just never know what animal or human can just pop out of nowhere in front of your vehicle. But, you also drive slowly because the roads are so bad and you would break your car in half if you went quickly. There is one spot that is particularly bumpy and when you go past this section of the road it is pretty much a single lane of traffic since there is a giant crater on one side of the road. Everyone takes turns to get by and then you move on. The delay and slow travel is also an excuse to wave and say hello to everyone you pass. It's a very tiny community and you are simply expected to be polite and say hello. Once you go through the main part of town you go right around a sharp turn, near a pharmacy, on a section of the road that gets flooded when it rains and is incredibly dusty when it doesn't.

On this particular day there is a huge rig pulling a 40 foot container and trying to manoeuvre its way around this tight, bumpy corner. Peter looks and says "Ooh look, maybe it's ours!" Even though he knows it isn't because ours is coming next week. He then says for the hundredth time "I can't wait until we get our stuff!"

We watch as the driver stops and gets out of his cab and walks over to the next car behind him and speaks to that driver. This car is directly in front of us and since we are stuck in traffic (which is pretty funny for Trujillo because it is so small) we have nothing to do but watch.

I immediately think of those Malibu Rum commercials on TV where a bus has stopped somewhere on an island in the Caribbean. A man gets on the bus and says "you are late" and the driver says "I am not late". Then a passenger says "you are late". Another passenger stands up and says "you are two minutes late and now you are making me late!" The commercial ends with one man on a bicycle who is waiting behind the bus and he says "OH, NO... TOTAL GRIDLOCK!" It's a funny commercial, worth looking up on YouTube. It reminded me of the traffic jam we were in now. Three cars behind a truck in Trujillo makes a traffic jam!

The driver walks back to his cab and gets moving but, as he walks away I say to Peter "Man, that guy looks just like Joe who works for Roger. Really, those two could be brothers". Isn't it funny when people can remind you of other people even when you are in a remote town in Honduras? They say that everyone has a twin. Maybe that's true. In a few minutes we are back on the road back to the ranch which Roger always calls the house.

✳ August 18, 2008

This morning Roger's right hand guy Joe comes to the house and who is sitting beside him in the truck? The same guy that was driving the big rig yesterday! I smile and shake my head. I walk directly over to Joe and ask him if this is his brother. He says "yes". I ask the brother if he drives a large rig and he looks at me wondering how I know this. I tell him the story about seeing him yesterday and how I looked at his face and just thought how much he reminded me of Joe and that he could be his brother. Because he actually was!

We are all killing ourselves laughing and you realize just how small the world and the gene pool around here really is. If you see someone in Trujillo that looks like someone else and you wonder if they are brothers... chances are they probably are.

Peter went to have a rum and coke with Karl this evening. Karl lives next door and he is also the property manager for Roger's home and land. He makes sure things get fixed when they are broken and manages any work around the house. He also makes sure everything is ok when Roger is away or travelling. When Peter got back home he told me that Karl has a strict uniform. Karl is usually wearing pretty much the same type of thing every day unless he has to go into town. You can usually hear Karl coming. He wears sandals and you can tell it's him by his gait walking along the sand coated driveway. When you see him he is wearing shorts and sandals and that's it, that's the uniform. If he has to go to town he adds a shirt. This is called dressing up. At home he wears the shorts and the sandals. He has a variety of shorts but they are all the same style and he is very specific about those shorts. Karl and Judy told Peter how Karl just loves those shorts. They are called Stubbies. He loved them so much that he took them to a place to have 30 pairs made exactly the same. He was very proud of the fact that now he can wear them almost all of the time.

✳ August 19, 2008

Peter had to go into town today to see the lawyer. He has to give the lawyer the list of all our items in the shipping container. Yes, when you move to another country you need to list everything in your container. That means everything you have packed in each of your boxes gets listed. We have everything on a giant multi-page document and the lawyer needs this list so they can have someone translate it into Spanish for the port authorities to compare in order to clear customs. Peter walks in the lawyer's office and there are several guns on a big table and a guy is trying to sell them to the lawyer and six other guys looking at them. He looks at Peter and says "you want to buy a gun?" Peter looks at the guns and says "I am more of a 45 mm kind of guy, thanks". Two seconds later the guy whips out a couple of 45's! Peter looks at them and says "maybe I should wait to become a resident before a get myself a gun". The guy looks at him and says "ok!"

Peter is escorted into one of the lawyer's offices and waits. A few minutes pass and a woman walks in the front door and goes into the other office where the lawyer is at the moment. Peter hears "kissing" sounds, then a zipper and... you know the rest! How does Peter hear this so clearly? Well because there are two offices and a main outer room however, all the ceilings are open to the entire suite. Peter heard it and so did all the other guys in the front room looking at guns. You just never know what you will stumble upon on any given Tuesday morning in town. I imagine it's probably similar to lawyer's offices all over the place.

✳ August 20, 2008

On any given summer day near the equator, it's understood that it's going to be hot. I find that it is normally 28-30 degrees C and 60-80% humidity. This morning the power went off and there is a problem with the backup generator. This is a large house and there are maybe twenty ceiling fans that run constantly, plus seven large fans on floor stands. I find it incredibly hot with all the fans running and all the windows open. As soon as there is no power you realize just how hot it really is. It takes about four minutes and I start to really sweat. Water is just pouring off me. As I am writing this in my journal my arm is sticking to the paper.

Most Hondurans have no air conditioning, no fans and no screens on their homes. I realize you get acclimatized after a certain period of time and if you have always lived here chances are you adjust to it. I can't wait for that day to happen to me. I have to say I really do feel Canadian. We just do not sweat like this on a regular basis. Last night it was so hot that when I jumped in the pool, it felt as warm as bath water and I didn't find any relief. I am hoping I will get used to this because I am totally consumed with my overheated body and find it very difficult to think of anything else. I feel like those creepy, sweaty people who always have sweat on their upper lip and no one wants to shake their hand because they are just so damp. Just gross! I have become that guy!

Our shipping container arrived at the house this afternoon. I should have taken a picture of the rig pulling it. The front of the truck was all smashed up, the bumper was missing and the container was attached to the flatbed with a couple of chains. Yikes! With the roads the way they are it's a miracle that it made it. I am thrilled that it's here with all my worldly crap. It is amazing how your old personal belongings can bring you such comfort.

We got the container out of the port of Castilla within a record time of three days. That's pretty amazing for these parts. Apparently we also got a good break on duty since we only had to pay $3000 US to bring our old shit into the country. It seems pretty steep to me since the estimated value of our goods in total was $5000 but at this point I don't care. I am glad we finally have it and I want my things.

We hired ten guys to help us. It was 31 degrees C and 70% humidity and those guys were hustling their asses off. They spent their morning clearing the brush in the field in front of the house with machetes as part of their regular work and the afternoon unloading the truck. They carried all the boxes on their backs for some reason and were just pouring sweat. I still cannot believe we had all this shit in a 900 square foot house. We had to empty everything into the house in order for the container to be light enough to remove it off the truck. We tried to find some of the boxes we wanted to unpack into our room and it felt like Christmas because we found lots of things we were thrilled to have. We then positioned the empty container on the lawn near the garage and then we had to repack it all for storage until we have our own place. Thank God Peter is a master of packing things like a puzzle. The container will stay there until we have a house to move it into.

✳ August 21, 2008

There is a single strand of electrical wire that is hanging outside the doors that lead out to the patio from our bedroom. Tonight when I took the dogs out for a pee I noticed a little black and white sparrow perched on that wire sleeping. It's so odd to see this little bird sleeping out in the open, perfectly balanced on the single strand of wire. He is so cute and it is a moment of pure joy for me. I stand there for a few more minutes just watching and feeling my smile wrap me up.

Thank you for this feeling of happy.

✳ August 22, 2008

We went to Rogues Galleria on the beach road today for lunch. They have a cat that has some young kittens. There is one tiny, skinny black kitten that always comes around me whenever I am there. I call him Gato Negro and after I am done my lunch I always feed him a bit of anything I have left over. I always feel like I am selling drugs when I feed any stray animal here. I know they are hungry so my natural inclination is to feed something that is hungry especially when I have food. I also know that when they beg to other people some get very angry and scare them off or potentially worse. I am always so torn because I don't want to help and hurt them in the long run. Why can't I feed them all? For today no one is around and I feed him little pieces of my leftover chicken. I pick his scrawny little body up and put him on my lap and pet and scratch him. For three happy minutes we are in love and life is perfect.

Tonight I noticed that the little sparrow is back on the wire in front of my bedroom doors. I take out the dogs and we don't disturb him and as we go back inside I wish him a good night sleep and blow him a kiss.

✳ August 23, 2008

I went out at 5:15 this morning to take the dogs for a pee and the little sparrow was still there. I say "Good morning little sparrow". He opened his little eyes, stared at me for a minute and then flew away. Nice.

The other thing that was unusual this morning was the concert of dragonflies that surrounded us. They looked so pretty with their flapping wings and their pleasant buzzing sound on the wet steam coming off the lawn.

This morning is remarkable because there is only 60% humidity in the house and I feel almost normal again. OMG! I am not sticky and sweating. You have no idea how grateful I feel at being comfortable. I feel good in my own skin again. I am going to sit and meditate on this feeling and how happy I am at this very moment. Thank you. Thank you. Thank you.

Wow the little sparrow came back tonight to sleep on my wire. It is so silly but this little thing makes me feel so happy. I am pleased to just stand in his presence. He seems like a gift from the fairies sent to make me smile. It was a good day.

✳ August 24, 2008

Carly has been asking us to keep our eyes open while shopping and if we ever see a vacuum cleaner to buy it. It would seem like a simple request however, it is almost impossible to find one where we are in Honduras. First of all no one we ask even understands what we are looking for. They don't know what a vacuum cleaner is. I am sure most people do not have rugs or carpets so it would not be something most would have use for. We have checked in all the normal places. We checked the big department stores in the mall. The closest thing we found was called an H2O vacuum in one of those Everything on TV stores. It is essentially a steam vacuum and you don't want the carpets wet since things are wet enough here. I am amazed they have one of those stores here. You can buy some of the most bizarre, obscure items in that store and I can't find top soil or a lemon! We searched every normal place we could think of and the best we could find was a shop vac in the hardware store.

We were at the architect's office this afternoon going over some house plans for the new subdivision and we asked him if he could help us find a vacuum. He said that he also tried to find a vacuum a while ago and couldn't. After we were finished at his office we were going to go back and buy the shop vac when we decided to go next door to a store called The American Store. It stocks many American products for the ex-pats that live here. Mostly, it has convenience foods that you cannot buy in the local grocery stores. We looked at all the things they had and I was excited to discover some good pasta that I had to buy and as I turned down the first aisle, there in three dusty boxes were Eureka upright vacuums. Who would ever have looked here? We bought a blue upright Eureka vacuum with hepa filter. We were so excited at our luck. I cannot wait to get it home and try it out on the rugs in the living room.

Once we got back, I assembled the vacuum and tried it out on the first rug. I was thrilled when it worked like a dream. I was so giddy and my reactions were so excited you would have thought I was on an infomercial. I was laughing and taking pictures. If you looked at the carpet you would never have thought it was dirty because it is normally brushed and swept regularly. I ran the vacuum over a small portion of the carpet and I filled ¾ of the container. A few more passes over the rug and the canister was almost full. Holy shit! It was totally amazing. I emptied the canister and I did it again and again and once more. I was amazed and grossed out all at the same time. When I really looked at all the dirt and hair I had collected I almost barfed.

I had to call Carly back in Canada. We had to bask in this glorious moment together. We laughed our faces off and she explained that she had been looking for a vacuum for literally the last five years. Although the rugs have been swept and brushed on a regular basis no one has ever vacuumed them in five years! We were laughing at what losers we were for thinking this was the greatest thing ever and how happy this stupid thing was making us. Clean is so nice.

I waited until Peter came home to do the second carpet so he could see how much dirt you could collect. He moved all the furniture and we filled and emptied the canister twice. It is amazing what you can't always see.

I totally want one for my new house too!

✳ August 25, 2008

The bugs can be unusually large down here. Cockroaches can be 2 ½ inches long and flies are like the gigantic rubber flies that you buy in those old fashioned joke shops. For whatever strange reason, the mosquitoes are the only things that are smaller. I wonder why? Why are they are so much itchier than the mosquito bites I have ever had before and why do they stay itchy for so long. WHY? WHY? Is their venom more concentrated in this heat? Such torture!

Giant beetle

This beetle with a big old horn on its head is the size of your hand. The tiles are 13 inch by 13 inch. What a monster!

✳ August 26, 2008

Last night we had a power failure. When you have no air conditioning and no fans in your bedroom, within a few minutes you start to feel like a dog locked in a car. It is sweltering hot here even at night.

Peter hooked up my washing machine today. I did laundry in my own washer. Wooo hooo! I have a wonderful LG front loading pretty blue washer and dryer pair. We hooked it up because it is better than the washer Carly has and we can both use it until I move out and she gets a new one. Right now only the washer is hooked up and working. I hope we can get the dryer working in a few weeks too. The problem is finding a wall outlet to fit the dryer plug into. No one typically has a dryer so we can't find a plug. Once we find it and can have it installed we can use the dryer. I look forward to the day we can have fluffy, soft towels.

Honestly, the things that just absolutely turn me on!

✳ August 27, 2008

It was 32 degrees today and even the Hondurans acknowledge it is hot. I simply cannot believe it could get this hot and humid. I once again imagine all the Hondurans that live with no electricity, no fans, and no air conditioning. We went for a long, luxurious drive in the air conditioned truck and I fantasized about living in the car with the air on full, blowing in my face perhaps being so cool I would actually have to wear a sweatshirt. Even in our bedroom that has an air conditioner, it has only cooled to 28 degrees. I swear if I get the money I am buying a huge air conditioner for the main part of the house.

Peter hooked up our own TV in our bedroom tonight. The house has a TV that is located in the little living room right near the front door but, it gets extremely hot in there. Now that we have our TV we will be able to watch TV in a cooler room. We have brought our Canadian satellite dish with us. We thought if we continued to pay for the service back in Canada we could try to see if it will work down here. It would be so nice to get English TV if we can make it happen. If not then we will hook up to the local cable TV. There are only two channels in English (the Hallmark Channel and CNN). I must say I have watched a lot of sappy, good, clean family, made-for-TV movies since I have been here. "Gosh darn it Pa!"

We also brought down our Sirius satellite radio for the car. You can technically get the radio working but, we have an older model unit that seems to have a problem with the connection cables staying in the radio during our bumpy rides. It isn't working well and we might just have to admit defeat on this one and cancel the service.

✳ August 28, 2008

I absolutely drip with mosquito bites... No really! I know that is so gross to say but, I never hear the mosquitos and I never feel them until after the bite and since they are the itchiest bites ever I HAVE TO scratch them. Once I scratch them they turn into a weird blister and then break and ooze. I am a complete mess. They are everywhere. We installed the bed net and hung up the mosquito black light killers but, I continue to be mobbed. I must have malaria. The numbers are against me. I must have a million mosquito bites! Ok, I am lying. I must have a hundred, thousand mosquito bites.

✳ August 29, 2008

I planted some sprouts in my sprouting container yesterday and today they have already started to sprout. They will taste great in a salad or sandwich.

Isn't it odd that the name of the thing and the action are the same? Sprouts sprouting!

Peter went to the butcher shop in Trujillo today. I didn't even know there was a butcher in Trujillo. I say that loosely because it is a building with three freezers and some meat. This guy doesn't really understand the whole butchering and aging process as we know it in North America. Basically a cow is shot; they chop it up and sell the pieces as soon as possible. When they run out, they don't sell beef again until they get another cow in. They sometimes may have pieces of meat that they freeze and then they don't actually know which cuts they are. Peter came home with a bag with some meat in it. I am ashamed to admit it but, I am going to make hamburgers made from what I think is possibly beef tenderloin.

We don't typically eat beef from here because it doesn't have the texture or feel of beef that we are used to. Beef is normally very tough because a cow in Honduras needs to work hard to get enough food to eat. The tenderloin Pete brought home was all loose and wobbly and I needed him to help me clean it because I was so grossed out at touching it. Now, just to be clear, I am not usually squeamish about touching raw meat and Peter is the one who totally is. The two of us looked like complete morons, holding the meat with tongs and trying to clean it without touching it. We were laughing our heads off and holding back the desire to throw up at the same time. I don't know why it was so gross to me. Partly it was because it was so wobbly and partly I think it was because he brought the two beef tenderloins home in an open white plastic shopping bag, the kind with handles you put groceries in. And instead of having the meat wrapped in plastic wrap or on a tray it is just bloody and loose in the bottom of the bag. It was like Halloween and he said "Trick or Treat" and they said "Trick" and tossed in two raw pieces of meat in his plastic bag!

I am this close to becoming a vegetarian; too bad it's hard to find good vegetables here. I wanted to taste what the meat was like but I just could not bring myself to eat it as a steak once I saw it. I admit I was scared. I have my KitchenAid stand mixer and I have a meat grinder attachment. So I have decided to grind it and make burgers. I add some spices and olive oil to it. We grilled them and they seemed to be ok. We didn't get stomach aches but, now we are worried that maybe we have worms or some other charming parasite. Fuck, how will I sleep tonight? I know I am going to have scary dreams.

I think this experience has taught me that I prefer chicken or fish, even though there are times when you really crave a good streak. I saved every single scrap I cut off from that meat and cooked it to give to the watchmen's dogs. I am sure they never get beef. Most people don't eat beef here. I did slice a few pieces into steaks and put them into a Ziploc bag with a marinade and froze them. Maybe someday when I have forgotten this experience of seeing it in the bag and cleaning it maybe I will try it as a steak? I am kind of excited to have a few things frozen and to have a stash of food in the freezer. You would swear I grew up in the depression and have a fear of going hungry. Not that I couldn't stand to miss a meal from time to time!

✳ August 30, 2008

Ah cravings! I miss so many things now that I can't just get them. I miss whipped cream, yogurt, blueberries, strawberries, raspberries, blackberries, spinach — I really crave greens. I want mushrooms, a good steak, pork tenderloin, oranges, lemons (wow do I miss lemons!), grapefruit, sushi, pepperoni on pizza, homemade sausages full of spices, sweet potatoes and unsalted butter.

I planted some macadamia nuts today. Maybe they will grow. I bought them as well as some papaya seeds on my last trip to Hawaii a few months ago.

✳ August 31, 2008

We went to a restaurant last night and I ordered fish but, I forgot to ask for filetas. They gave me a whole fried fish - head and all. Yuck! I hate when my food looks back at me.

✳ September 1, 2008

My poor little Lulu has 2 mosquito bites on the bottom of her feet and they are driving her nuts. I know how that feels. Look at those red feet. Poor girl!

My poor Lulu

Today I made some quinoa (that I brought from Canada), veggies, rice and grilled chicken. Maybe I will also make some bread. I have a huge watermelon. Perhaps I will make some watermelon daiquiris or margaritas. You get very creative here. If you want something that is not easily available you have to grow it, make it or forget it!

✳ September 2, 2008

There were three lovely horses on the beach this morning in front of the house. They were just standing under a small tree. There were two adult horses and one pony. All were a pretty caramel colour and when Lulu and I went for our early morning walk, Lulu didn't bark at them and they were not scared off by us.

When I walk on the beach I always look to see the dolphins. I look every day and never see any but, I know they are there.

A neighbor brings their cows to the property every morning to graze on the tall weeds in the field near the house. In North America most people would fence in their fields and move the cows from one area to another on their own property. The people in this area move their cows from place to place so they can get enough food. Once they have cleared a field they go to another.

Roger doesn't mind them being here because they keep the brush down and he doesn't have to pay guys to clear it with machetes. It has a benefit for the farmer and for Roger. There is a partial fence that separates the cows from the front of the house however, the watchmen are forever yelling at them when then sneak around. The cows try to sneak around because at the front of the house is the great big mango tree.

✳ September 3, 2008

Offering: noun

The act of presenting a gift or contribution
A presentation made to a deity as an act of religious worship or sacrifice; an obligation

I fed a mango to a cow today! This morning I picked up a couple of mangos and slowly walked over to the fence. I handed the mango through the fence to this nice cow and she ate it right out of my hand. Now this may not seem like a big deal however, most animals here are afraid of people. I am sure they are afraid of people for good reason. People yell at them, throw rocks at them or hit them with sticks to make them move. I understand cows are a commodity. They are not pets however I am always saddened when I see any farmer here or in Canada who feels they must treat their animals with unnecessary unkindness or cruelty. For me personally this is a true heartbreak. Many people feel this heartache for children or women who are abused. This is my personal arrow in the heart.

Ghandi said "The greatness of a nation and its moral progress can be judged by the way its animals are treated."

Basically if you look at a place and how it treats its weakest members will determine its greatness.

I think all nations have a way to go. We can all get better. In Honduras just managing to care for its people is hard. Animals are not really even a thought in terms of priority.

✳ September 4, 2008

I was gardening today. I was digging around in the sandy soil along the front driveway and all of a sudden a little crab just popped out of the sand and scared me. I don't mean it frightened me, I was just startled. Then another one popped out. You see lots of holes and where there are holes there are usually crabs.

They are just little blue crabs but it is funny to be digging and planting and all of a sudden a crab pops out! I was moving some oyster plants that were overcrowded in the other flower beds. These are fast multiplying spiky plants with a green leaf and purple underside. I dug up about a hundred of the plants and decided to transplant them to the grass area just surrounding the front driveway. I had moved some croton bushes and hibiscus shrubs and thought these low plants could be a nice ground cover under the shrubs.

The soil is pure sand and it doesn't look pretty, so this would cover it nicely. I was trying to make the planting around the driveway look more orderly. The workers that are around the property do not understand why I am doing this work. Maybe they think I should be asking them to do it. They come up to me and ask me why I am doing this and when I say I like to garden they think that is very unusual and walk away laughing. I look at my work when I am completed and realize how much we do for no other reason than it looks pretty. Part of me thinks we have gone to extremes in so many examples focusing on what others think but, I also look at what I have created and realize that I need beauty in my life just for how it feeds me. The plants are beautiful and they look lovely around the driveway. I know beauty holds another purpose in people's lives. It is important to surround yourself with things you feel are beautiful in order to feed your soul and your inspiration. I need to be inspired to create, to do more than just eat and live. That's why museums, art galleries and botanical gardens are important. We need to dream, to imagine, to be inspired and to simply be moved.

✳ September 5, 2008

There was another power failure today. Lately, there has been at least one per week, and sometimes it is more often. The watchmen will normally crank up the generator to let you have some electricity in order to do what is necessary at meal times. The last couple of weeks there has been a problem with the generator's battery so we have not had any backup. We just have to wait it out. It's at those moments when you really, really appreciate the work of the fans, as inadequate as they may seem normally.

✳ September 6, 2008

On the long drive to San Pedro Sula you will see many interesting things. You will see the large Dole commercial banana plantations. There are miles and miles of bananas. Then you pass miles of palm trees and all the trucks loading palm kernels which then are destined to become palm oil. You drive past rows upon rows of pineapples. There is even a little stretch that has rambutans which are a fuzzy red fruit in the lychee family. There are women who sit under a long stretch of canopied trees selling their plastic bags of fuzzy rambutans or breadfruit, which I must try one day.

We encounter a slowdown in traffic just as we pass the ladies selling. When we slow down and start passing we realize there is a long line of cars, some with their four way flashers on and people just walking in between the cars on the highway. At the front of the line we see a pickup truck with a casket in the back and people riding along with the casket. Each person is sitting on the side of the bed of the truck in the same pose. Head in hand making it clear that they are grieving. When cars drive by they all look up and then in unison they revert back to the same pose. It was really quite odd to see this dance of heads all doing the same thing at the same time.

We drive on.

You are driving 60–80 km/h and there are always dogs that just seem to jump out. I am a very nervous passenger on this road because I am so convinced we are going to hit something. At night I simply cannot look. You will be driving along and there are horses just walking along the side of the road with cars just whipping past them. I find the drive utterly nerve wracking and most of the time I just turn away from the road or close my eyes to avoid the scary sights. It's almost like those horror rides at the fair where you think someone is going to jump out and scare you.

✳ September 7, 2008

We drove to La Ceiba today. As we drive in I notice it looks like any city with its shopping malls, Wendy's and Pizza Hut restaurants, hotels and people all hustling and bustling. I look over at the road and see cars right alongside a horse pulling a cart. It reminds me of the car pool lanes in L.A. except instead of cars in that lane they have horses and carts and people just walking. Farther along we see chickens and pigs walking along going someplace on the same path.

✳ September 8, 2008

When you drive through Trujillo in the summer you often see women walking down the streets with big curlers in their hair (especially on Fridays, *gotta look hot on date night!*) or you see women walking around with a tea towel or a hand towel draped on their heads, like a hat to keep the sun off. The younger girls obviously think this is not cool and many of them just carry an umbrella. The men also have a strange fashion. The men fold the bottom of their shirts up to their underarms to expose their stomachs when it is hot. You will see them all happily walking down the street trying to keep cool just like that. Peter walks around in front of me like that around the house just to make me laugh.

How many people can you have on a local bus if the capacity is 50? I can guarantee you it will be a hell of a lot more than 50. People can stand in the aisles, they can hang off the back, and they will hang out the door. I am surprised they don't allow people to use the roof! Trucks are like that too. There are lots of pickup trucks and if you are driving down the street, and especially down a long dirt road, it is understood that you will stop for people along the way. If there is a woman and kids – always! You stop and she tells you where she is going and then they all hop in the back. I have seen 15 people in the back of a pickup. Most people just sit on the edge and hold on. The roads here are bumpy and you are amazed that more people don't fall out. I have even seen dump trucks full of people peaking over the back. A ride is a valuable thing!

I find this even funnier… They have seatbelt laws here. So if you come across a police checkpoint on the road, they are going to stick their heads in to see if you are wearing your seatbelt. But the 6 guys hanging off the back of the truck are ok. On your way now!

✳ September 9, 2008

I was walking down the hall from my bedroom to the kitchen this morning and there was a scorpion just happily walking down the same path. I ran and got the biggest, heaviest catalogue I had in my bedroom and squished him dead. I then decided it was important to jump and stomp on top of the catalogue for good measure. I felt quite brave killing that scorpion all by myself. Just me and that catalogue! I couldn't let him go about his business when my Molli and Lulu walk down those same halls. I did however leave the catalogue there for Peter to dispose of said scorpion when he came home. I also had to show him what I had done like a child who has a poop and must proudly show it to his father. Look what I did! TA DA! Peter laughed at me and when he removed the catalogue he found the dead scorpion and wondered what I had done since that scorpion was as flat as a sheet of paper. All I could say was "TA DA!"

My little garden project is coming along. I have to start the seeds indoors in my little pots with the seed starter mix Peter bought for me. Then I place my little pots on giant cookie trays in Roger and Carly's shower. They are not here right now and their shower has glass blocks which gets some early morning sun and is the only sunny window in the house. I can't leave my tiny containers outside because if it rains, it rains big heavy buckets and squishes everything. Once they are a few inches high, I can transplant them to my flower bed which is raised and close to the kitchen window as well as covered partially by the roof. My basil is coming along and my Swiss chard and spinach are starting but they are still struggling since they are plants that typically grow in colder weather and this place is anything but cold. I am so desperate to have a spinach salad or some Swiss chard I ask them nicely if they will please grow just as a special gift for me. I could pray but, I figure I will need prayers for the bigger stuff that is bound to happen.

✳ September 10, 2008

I have planted some 4 o'clock (Mirabilis) flower seeds along the driveway. They are pretty flowers that open every day at 4 o'clock. Peter came home today with a present for me…Terra Negro (black soil). I am so excited. Who knew you could buy me a bag of dirt and I would think it was a great gift? I have also brought Miracle Grow fertilizer from Canada. The flowers just love it. I would never use it on food but the flowers do very well with it. I mix it in my watering can and the guards all ask me what I am doing. I tell them it's vitamins to feed the plants and now they think they have seen it all. You feed the plants too? It is confirmed, I am nuts.

✳ September 11, 2008

There are infomercials here just like at home except the products are not ones I have ever seen before. The one I see all the time now is "Jeans UP!" It is a pair of jeans that makes your flabby bum bigger and higher. I understand the perkier part but, I don't normally buy a pair of pants to make my ass bigger! Honey do these make my ass look big? Great, that's what I was going for.

This afternoon I heard a banging noise and went out to the pool area to investigate. This little green lizard was trying to get through a small hole in the stand of the pool filter. (The lizard was larger than a gecko but not big like the black and white iguanas that run around the lawn). He got halfway in and there he stayed stuck. He was flipping and banging to try to free himself. I tried to think of some way to help him get unstuck but I really had no idea what I could possibly do. Peter said we should just leave him and he would probably figure it out. A few hours later I came out to see if he was still there and he was gone. So he either wiggled his way free or something ate him! I am just glad we didn't have to lop him in half to get him out.

I made my own mustard today. I had some mustard seeds that I brought from Canada and although I can buy that bright hot dog mustard in La Ceiba, I wanted some nice mustard so I decided to make my own.

Beer Mustard

½ cup of mustard seeds

¾ cup flat beer

1 tbsp. mustard powder

1 tbsp. onion powder

1 tsp. dried thyme

½ cup cider vinegar

2 tbsp. honey

1 tsp. salt

- In a small bowl soak mustard seeds in beer for 24 hours. Stir in remaining ingredients. Blend in a blender until some seeds are ground and others still are whole. Place in a glass jar and store in fridge for 1 week before using. It will continue to absorb liquid and get thicker over time.

This afternoon while we were cleaning the truck in the car port, Lulu decided she was going to hop up on the quad and sit on the seat. That dog wouldn't sit on the concrete for nothing! SNOB!

What a princess!

✳ September 13, 2008

Roger had some habanero peppers in the freezer. There were about a ½ pound of peppers plus these teeny tiny little chillies that Judy had grown for him. Habaneros, or scotch bonnets, are some of the hottest peppers on earth. Carly wouldn't even touch them. Honestly, if you even touch your hands to your mouth with a speck of that pepper juice on it you will know it. I was wondering what you would do with these frozen peppers. If they were fresh you could grill them. I decided to go online and see if I could make my own hot sauce. The recipe I found that I liked on the web was called "Sun of a beach hot sauce" which I thought was quite fitting. Joe always says "SUN NA MA BEECH" when he is mad about something. So this was the hot sauce for me. This is a Caribbean based hot sauce and it is extremely HOT!!

I modified the recipe and created this concoction.

RJ's Triple XXX Hot Sauce

2 cups of frozen habanero/scotch bonnet peppers - seeds and stems removed
(cause that will make it milder- who are you kidding here!)

1 green pepper- seeded/chopped

1 onion – chopped in quarters

4 cloves garlic- crushed

2 mangos

1 tomato - chopped

½ cup lime juice

½ cup cider vinegar

1 tbsp. fresh basil - chopped fine

2 tbsp. orange juice

1 tbsp. fresh parsley - chopped fine (or cilantro)

2 tbsp. sweet mustard (like a honey mustard) OR 2 tbsp. regular Dijon mustard and 2 tbsp. honey

½ tsp. ground nutmeg

1 tsp. salt

Whenever you are cleaning and removing seeds from habaneros do so with gloves and be extremely careful. These are truly hot peppers. I used plastic bags on my hands so I would not touch them.

- In a food processor, add habanero peppers, green pepper, onion, garlic, mangos and tomato. Pulse until pureed. Be careful when you remove the mixture from the food processor, don't breathe in the aroma from the peppers or you will be very sorry!

- Add to a bowl: the peppers that you pureed, lime juice, cider vinegar, chopped basil and parsley, orange juice, mustard, honey, nutmeg and salt. Mix and carefully put in a sealed bottle in the fridge.

It will last forever in the fridge.

Once it was done I just touched the sauce to my lips and it burned for 15 minutes. (I timed it!) How does anyone put that on their food without rotting their stomach?

I made a stir fry with chicken, peppers, coconut milk, and onions. I added a ½ a demi - tsp. of that hot sauce and it was perfectly spicy for us. Any more would have been suicide. Even that small amount and you could really taste the heat!

Roasting: verb

To expose to great or excessive heat. To cook in an oven or near hot coals.
A tribute or banquet in which the honouree is both praised and insulted.

I made some really good pork loin today. We got the pork from the big market in La Ceiba. I roasted it in orange juice. (There were some ripe oranges near the gate – I have never been here before when we could eat them. They are some kind of wild orange and they are not pretty but they did the job.) I also used lime juice – we have a lime tree outside the front door near the mango tree. I made it like Cuban pork. I served it with some sauce I made from cider vinegar, barbeque sauce and some Latin spices to make it nice and moist. We ate it with warm tortillas and some lettuce and tomatoes. Served with cold beers it was terrific. Hmmm… Maybe next time I get some pork I can make my own sausages. I have the sausage attachment for the KitchenAid. They would be good grilled!

Cuban Style Pork Loin

3-4 lb. pork loin – butterfly to open flat

½ cup orange juice

½ cup lime juice

2 tbsp. lime zest

2 tbsp. olive oil

1 tbsp. cumin

1 tsp. pepper

1 onion - cut in quarters

4 cloves garlic

1 tbsp. fresh cilantro (I had to grow mine because they only have culantro here)

1 tbsp. dried oregano

1 tsp. salt

- In a large Pyrex dish add orange juice, lime juice, lime zest, 2 cloves garlic crushed. Stir and add meat. Cover with plastic wrap and leave to marinate at least 8 hours.

- Remove the meat from liquid and pat dry. Leave the juices in the pan.

- In a food processor, add onion, crushed garlic, cumin, pepper, cilantro, oregano and salt. It will make a rough paste. Spread ½ the paste on the inside of the meat. Roll up and tie with string. Rub the remaining paste over outside of roast.

- Chop another onion or two and place in the Pyrex dish to form a bed. Place the pork on top of onions and cook in a 325 degree oven for 2 ½ -3 ½ hours. I like to cook it covered with foil for the first hour so that the juices in the bottom of the pan steam the meat. Then I cook the rest of the time uncovered, basting it approximately every ½ hour. You can also turn it every half hour for the first hour and a half. The goal is to have the meat become fall apart tender. Ideally this is done with pork shoulder but, I had a pork loin with some fat on it and it worked out great.

- Let the pork rest for ½ hour before slicing or pulling apart. It makes great sandwiches or you can serve it sliced with rice and a crisp salad. We had it pulled in tortillas and it was sensational. Joe stayed for dinner and I served my Cuban pork tortillas with lettuce and tomatoes and some ice cold beers. Having a good meal is challenging but brings me such satisfaction and nourishes my soul as well as my body.

✳ September 15, 2008

I made some really good ginger spice cookies with fresh ginger which I was happy to see in the market. I had some ground ginger and some crystallized ginger which I brought with me from Canada. The cookies were very strongly ginger flavoured rolled in sugar and very yummy. I find baking makes me feel more at home and is so nice to share with others.

Three-way Ginger Cookies

2 1/4 cups flour

2 tsp. ground powdered ginger

2 tsp. baking soda

1/2 tsp. ground cinnamon

1/2 tsp. salt

1/2 cup very finely chopped crystallized ginger

1/2 cup packed dark brown sugar

1/2 cup white sugar

1 cup unsalted butter – room temperature (if you are in Honduras use the salted butter and leave out the 1/2 tsp. salt in the recipe)

1 large egg- room temperature

1/4 cup molasses

2 tbsp. fresh grated ginger

1/2 cup icing sugar or course sugar to roll cookies in

- Combine flour, ground ginger, baking soda, ground cinnamon, crystallized ginger and salt in a bowl and set dry ingredients aside. Using an electric beater, mix brown sugar, white sugar and butter until fluffy approximately 4 minutes on high in another bowl. Add egg and molasses and fresh ginger to the sugar mix until blended. Add the dry ingredients to the wet and mix until just combined. Cover and refrigerate 1 hour.

- Heat your oven to 350 degrees F. Lightly, butter baking sheet or use a sheet of parchment paper. Put ½ cup of icing or white sugar in a bowl. Form dough into balls; roll in white sugar to coat completely. Place cookies on baking sheet 2 inches apart. Bake 12 minutes, until cracked on top but still soft to the touch.

❋ September 16, 2008

Today I made some quick rice pudding with rice, milk, coconut milk, cinnamon, sugar, and shredded coconut. I thought it was delicious; Peter thinks rice pudding is totally gross. So...I ate it all myself.

The cleaning lady came today. We pay her 150 lempira a day. Apparently we are in trouble because we give her 50 lempira more than the other cleaning ladies get around here so we are making other people look bad. By the way, 150 lempira is $7.50 for a full day. We explained that we don't provide lunch like the other people do. This is a small place and you do not want to upset the natural order of things.

❋ September 17, 2008

Peter was in La Ceiba today and he took the new guy named Juan with him as a translator. They decided to stop at the Wendy's in the mall for a quick lunch. Juan had never been to a Wendy's before so this was a new experience. They were up at the counter and Peter was asking him what he wanted. After choosing he asked him if he wanted to supersize his meal. Juan didn't know what that meant however, if someone is offering you food in a poor country you say yes, so he said yes. He was shocked when he received his bucket of coke and his giant hamburger. Peter is used to being in North America where we are always in a rush and he ate his meal in 5 minutes and was ready to go. Whenever you go to La Ceiba you are always rushing to get everything you want done before it gets dark. There are always so many things you want to do when you come to town and things usually take longer than you expect. Juan was shocked at how quickly Peter finished his meal and was struggling to eat his fast. He didn't want to leave anything on his plate but, this was a huge meal for such a little guy. Peter was impatient and so Juan rushed and finished eating quicker than he normally would. In the end Peter said Juan was looking pretty green and uncomfortable. We just take for granted that there will always be a next meal and if we are full we just throw away what we don't want. Wendy's is not my idea of a great meal but, it does make you think how gross the North American portions are and how hard it is for us to just slow down.

❋ September 18, 2008

There are large, yellow tailed Orioles nesting under the ceramic roof tiles on the pool side of the house. It is good protection from the rain for their babies but, I cannot imagine how they can stand the excruciating heat that must exist in there. They make a big mess on the back deck but they are so funny because it sounds like they are saying "eat yer meat!" So we just call them the "eat yer meat" birds.

✳ September 19, 2008

I went on a big road trip with Al today. We had to go to San Pedro Sula which is approximately 5 hours away. We were meeting with two distributors to look at things for the new homes we are building. Al is coming along to drive me there and also to translate and help me ask the questions I need answered from each company. He is Honduran born however, his father was American and his mother is Honduran. He is 68 years old and is very formal. He reminds me of a formal British person and even speaks with a British accent, which seems odd to me. You would never imagine he was Honduran. He reminds me of Peter O'Toole's character in Club Paradise – a funny old movie from the '80s.

We drove the long distance in his truck, stopping each hour so he could stretch his legs, buy a drink, or use the facilities at the gas stations along the way. It was a very strange drive because for the majority of the time we didn't speak at all. There was no radio on and we basically sat in silence unless I saw something I could ask him about. There were a few occasions where he would voluntarily give me some information about the Dole pineapple plantation or the railroad that was built in 1963 to transport the pineapples. He would tell me about the ladies selling lychees (really they were rambutans - he just called them lychees) or breadfruit. So, other than a few discussions, it was pretty quiet in the car.

When we arrived in San Pedro we stopped by his house, which is five minutes outside of town and dropped off his stuff. He basically ran in and ran out again so he didn't keep me waiting. We drove to the Grand Sula Hotel where I will be staying while we are in town. He dropped me off and told me he will be back to pick me up in 2 hours.

It is a Best Western Hotel and when I walk into the lobby it looks fine. Nothing fancy but ok. I check in and go to my room - 617. All along the hallway to my room are folded rollaway beds and it looks like I am in the hallway of a school or an institution built in the '60s. I am not getting a warm and fuzzy feeling.

This is the hallway outside my room. Warm and inviting...if you are going to prison!

The bed is old. The bedspread... I am scared to imagine what has happened on that fabric. I am positive no one has ever washed it.

I remove the bedspread and flop on the gross bed and just cry. I am so unhappy.

There is a loud window air conditioner beside the bed. The washroom makes me feel like I have walked into a basement apartment owned by bachelor. You know the kind... they don't believe they need to clean. If they close the shower curtain no one will ever notice. I feel trapped. I feel forced to be where I don't want to be. I am in a gross '70s hotel room with dark and dingy furniture. God, I am surprised the bed didn't take coins. I am not normally a germaphobe but, in hospitals, airplanes and gross hotel rooms I can snap right into one.

That night I slept in my clothes. I wore jeans and socks and put a towel on my pillow. I prayed the bleach would kill or keep away anything that might be living in the pillow. I wrapped myself in my T-shirt because I wouldn't get under the sheet. When the air conditioner came on I froze and woke up. When it turned off I was sweating and dying of heat. I kept the lights on all night long because who knows what could come out in the dark.

I can see how people can get crazy out of control with their phobias. There is no logic involved when you are freaking out. I will be sure to point out that they did have a nice, new Samsung flat screen TV when I write my Travelocity review.

I have always known that I am a hotel snob. I do not believe in the saying that "it is just a place to sleep. Who cares?" NO not true!

In the morning I felt like I had made it through the night in a haunted house and survived. I have never been camping in my life either but, I just know I wouldn't like sleeping in a tent and using disgusting shared facilities with other drunk party people. I am just not that kind of girl. I was only too happy to shower (with a towel on the floor of the shower so I wouldn't touch the tiles) and get the hell out of there!

I go downstairs and see if I can eat the breakfast that is included with the room. It's an ok looking sort of café. Since I am not into eggs I order toast, coffee and orange juice. The toast is fine and the coffee is really strong but good. The juice comes in those tiny little shot glasses they used to serve you orange juice in the '70s and surprisingly the colour of the juice is green! The taste is perfectly like orange juice but it is so strange and unattractively green.

We go to our first distributor. My job is to go through a ten page spreadsheet and detail by detail pick tiles, taps and sinks that would appeal to a North American buyer. I am looking for three standard choices and three upgraded choices. It seems simple enough.

Well, if you went to the Home Depot or any large chain in North America you could do it. You walk up to the taps and you look at the choices. You find three that are in the same price range with different looks and finishes and mark down the item numbers and costs. It's a big job but I was hoping ok, maybe I could do it in 4 hours.

We made an appointment and we have a person dedicated to helping us for as long as necessary. He is nice and speaks a little English and Al is there to help me. First thing to mention is there is no air conditioning and we are in a huge, HUGE showroom and warehouse. It's hot and noisy. They are renovating part of the show-room and then it hits you… They are putting down some kind of flooring and there is this extremely strong, toxic odour coming from the glue they are using.

I start with tiles. I look at bathroom tiles. Ok, I like one called Azulex-Orion. It comes in white, beige and grey. Ok. I write down the numbers and I ask "how much?" He has to go and check each one individually in the computer at the other end of the store. Their system is numbers based and they must enter each number individually into the system in order to find a price. It cannot bring up all three at the same time because they are all the same tile in multiple colours. I wonder why all three aren't the same number with "w, b, and g" at the end of the number to indicate color? Why don't they have it in the system by name as well so you could find all similar tiles with the same pattern? So, we wait and 5 minutes later he says here is the price and the white is available but the grey and the beige are not. I ask what does this mean? Will they be getting more? Are these colors discontinued? He says "who knows?" Ok, so why do they have them on display? I try another three choices and each time some are not available. I think this is nuts! How can I give homeowners a choice if they will never be guaranteed that we can get those choices? I think how will I ever get through my list today? I decide that rather than ask him to look up each number which is taking forever, I will go through my list and choose what I can, writing down all the numbers and colors and I will email them the list from home. They can then provide me with the costs and tell me if they are available or not. The guy that works there says yes he can do that. I go through my items one by one, choosing different items in similar price ranges. There are a few items with prices on them but, he helps me guess which ones are in similar price ranges and so we guess most of the list. I choose three standard choices and three upgraded choices. It is such a ridiculous way to do this.

I also have a list of items from our architect like rebar and other building materials that I need pricing on. The rebar has a number to indicate the thickness of the rebar. They say #4, #5, etc. The supplier doesn't know what this rebar is because they have a different numbering system. Why, am I not surprised? I call Peter to help because I don't know shit about rebar or the sizes. He is able to clarify for me the different sizes of rebar and the guy helping finds their associated numbers in their system. I ask if they sell mortar for the tiles and he says "what's that? Is it the same as concrete?" And so on, and so on.

After three hours, water is running down my back and face like a river. Al has to sit down because he is high from the glue we have been sniffing. The guy that works in the place looks at me and says "you look really tired." Yeah, no shit! In the end, I just don't have it in me to ask for any supplies related to foundations or anything structural. I focused all my time on toilets and finishes. When we finally leave and get into Al's truck. We were both just hovering over the air conditioning vent like it was a drink. You have no idea how utterly orgasmic it was to be in that truck with Al. I never thought I would use the word orgasmic and Al in the same sentence in my life!

He drops me off at the hotel and says he will pick me up tomorrow at 8 am.

I drop off my junk in my room. I am *thrilled* about spending another *wonderful* night in this place. I walk across the street to see what I can eat for dinner. The hotel has a restaurant but, it's a little too scary for me to attempt. I have had enough new experiences for one day thanks. I walk across the street and then through a park to get to some restaurants. First I find a pharmacia to get something for my exploding head. Everything in the store is behind the counter and I ask her in my bad Spanish for something for my "capesa". I hand motion and ask for Tylenol or Advil and she says yes she has Advil. She puts a tiny package on the counter with 2 Advil sealed inside. I ask if I can have a bottle and she gives me another tiny package with 2 Advil. At this point I don't care and have no fight left in me. I pay my 30 lempira ($1.50) and leave.

I head towards every gross chain restaurant that I would never normally eat at. There is KFC, Dunkin Donuts, Burger King, McDonalds and Pizza Hut. I choose Pizza Hut. I order a veggie personal pan pizza and a bottle of water. I sit in the waiting area at the front of the restaurant and watch all the people coming and going and finally my order is ready. I haven't been to Pizza Hut in years but when did the personal pan pizza become the size of the cakes I used to bake in my Easy Bake Oven? My dinner costs 60 lempira ($3.00). At least I can say I am not spending a lot of money!

I take my pizza and my water back to my hotel room and eat it while watching "Nine Months" with Hugh Grant. There is usually one thing on in English and that's it, take it or leave it. I took it.

After I finish eating I put another towel on the floor in my shower and hose myself down. I step out and notice a big long black hair on my floor. My hair is not black and is not that long. My mind immediately goes to the hotel manager who I am imagining taking his girlfriend to my room to have sex in my bathroom before I got back today. I am grossed out. I put on my clothes so I can sleep another night in this swell joint. I call Peter to explain all the antics from that day and laugh at how funny it all is. Thank God I have him to vent to. I then go downstairs to the bar and buy 2 Port Royal beers, which are pretty good by the way, and I am not even a beer drinker. I take my bottles up to my room and watch the very first or second episode of Grey's Anatomy. (I think in real life they are on season 6?? But I could be wrong.) I am glad I never watched it so it's a new episode to me. I fall asleep after the show and then spend the rest of the night waking up every time I hear the air conditioner come on.

※

The next day I am happy and excited because I get to check out. I go downstairs for my toast, coffee and green orange juice and we are off to the next distributor.

On the way I notice all the cars and horses with carts. There are lots of people begging here or selling things. They walk up to your car when you are stopped at lights. One woman completely breaks my heart. I could not believe the sight of her and had to literally shut my mouth from gawking. She was approximately 50 if I had to guess. She was limping and had some kind of patch over one eye. Where her mouth should be was a hole. She had no lips and had a white crust around the entire hole. From this white hole she was just pouring saliva. I have literally never seen anything like it in my life. I wondered what her story could possibly be. What could have happened to her? I ask Al what he thought could have happened to her and he says nonchalantly "some disease" like he sees this kind of thing every day. Maybe he does.

I think of that woman for the rest of the day. I simply cannot fathom in a country that has public medical help available for free, how it is possible that she could not get some help somehow? She lives in the city so she can get to the hospital which is sometimes the biggest challenge for the people that live in remote areas. How is it that there isn't one person that she knows, that could help her in some way?

On the drive home Al says that sometimes when families have members with illnesses or disabilities they simply get outcast and many of them just end up living on the streets begging. This country just makes me feel so horrible sometimes. The problems are so numerous and so complex .There are no easy solutions. This is many years in the making and progress is slow for many reasons as well. It is not as simple as throwing money at the issues because the country has been getting assistance from other countries for years. The country needs to shift consciousness on so many levels and create workable solutions for themselves with the help of other countries but not just simply by getting handouts which causes many issues as well. You are dammed if you do and dammed if you don't. So much of what I see is just heartbreaking. You really do not have any idea unless you travel to see some of the issues we don't even imagine in developed countries.

We get to the next showroom and it is fantastic, like night and day compared to my visit yesterday. It's beautifully laid out. The products are gorgeous and the people are friendly and helpful. You go from one extreme to another in Honduras. The guy who is helping me speaks English perfectly. He was educated in Miami and his uncle is one of the owners of the showroom. He is interested in his business and likes what he is doing. It is really so nice to see a man in his 20s that is excited about life and what he is going to do in the world. In Honduras this is even more impressive. In the last few years I have to say that even in Canada there are so many young people already discouraged by the world and their place in it. I feel like so many just want to go straight to retirement. They are not excited about anything. When I was in my 20s I just want to get promoted and make money. I had something to prove and people to show I could do whatever I put my mind to. There was no apathy in my 20s, just enthusiasm and raw ambition.

We easily go through our list and get prices in the time we have allotted. The salesman has to check some items for availability but, it's much more thorough than the supplier we went to yesterday. We have to go to their other location to see some door locks and hardware. Since we want to head home from the other location he takes his own truck and we follow him. He gets into his vehicle and his bodyguard comes with him. You realize that although you are in a beautiful showroom in a big city because this country has such extreme poverty those who "have" are a constant target for those who so desperately "have not". We look at the other products and once done we head back towards Trujillo.

San Pedro Sula to Trujillo is a good five hour drive and it gets dark every day at 6 pm. (You have light from 6 am to 6 pm all year round when you live at the equator.) It is 12 noon and Al is so happy we are on our way. He was almost desperate when he explained we had to leave early. I tried my best to get through the second showroom and once we were on the highway he happily explained that he can't see at night. So it's a good thing we left when we did. Sight is kind of a requirement if you are a driver, don't *ya* think? I am glad we are on our way too.

The drive back is even quieter than the way there. There is once again no radio on in the car and Al is not as talkative as he was on the way to San Pedro. I can sense that he just wants to get there. He wants to get some gas and tells me that I should just tell him when I want to eat something and he will stop. He makes his first stop early at a gas station that has a small buffet cafeteria. He doesn't explain that this is the stop for food he is talking about and pretty much there is nothing until you get to La Ceiba which is three hours away. He gets out and gets gas. He comes back with two chocolate bars. He eats both bars like a hungry wolf and I say to him we can stop any time he wants if he wants to have lunch but, I am fine for the time being. We drive another hour and he makes another stop at a gas station where he stretches his legs and says that he doesn't want to stop for lunch so I say ok. I want to get home too.

I buy a bag of chips and we get going. We pass hour after hour in silence.

At 4:30 pm, a switch turns on in his head and he starts to get excited. He is thanking me for moving it and not stopping for lunch. Then he gets a phone call. He takes the call, says a few ok's, fine and hangs up. I don't ask and he says "that was my girlfriend". I smile and think he was talking to his wife and think "isn't he cute". Ten minutes later he gets another call and says a few ok's, fine and hangs up. I don't ask and he says "that was the boss!" and laughs. It was at this point when I realize this was his wife and he does have a girlfriend. Holy shit, Al you old rooster!

In between La Ceiba and Trujillo we stop on the side of the road and Al buys some rambutans. He places the bags of fuzzy fruit on the seat between us. It's 5 pm when we drive into Trujillo. As we approach the main part of town he points to a house we pass and says "that's my girlfriend's house and she wanted the lychees". He drops me off at Rogues Galleria on the beach road and I call Peter to tell him to come meet me because now I am starving! Al parks the car and decides he wants a drink. He sits down next to me at the bar and says he is going to meet his girlfriend here. We each order a cold beer and all of a sudden he jumps up and says "I like everything bad for me! I like booze and sex and lobster and meat!" He then gets up and says "I am going to get my girlfriend and we will be back for dinner!" And then in a second he is gone.

I look at Lucita, the owner, and we both just burst of laughing! I say "I don't know who that was! I don't know what just happened! I just spent two full days in a car driving with that man who spoke maybe 10 minutes of that whole time. This is a man that is almost twice my age and called me ma'am the whole time. Now I just met his alter ego "Al the Stud!" Honduras definitely turns any man a certain level of macho.

I dare you to test this theory. It's the wild, wild, west and men just go all caveman here. It is very noticeable. Even the mildest mannered man will someday surprise you and you will look over and say "Who are you?"

❋ September 21, 2008

There are 6 giant hibiscus bushes in the middle of the field directly in front of the main house. Peter asked the watchmen to move them whenever they had time. He explained that today the soil is very dry and maybe they should water them and then loosen the soil from around the bush and then move them tomorrow, no rush. He knew they were big plants and it is hot out and he didn't want them to overexert themselves and get hurt. We walk back into the kitchen and two minutes later the watchmen are already re-planting them around the driveway. It takes all three of them to do it but, they move them right away. These guys work really hard in this heat and I am very thankful for their help. These were large bushes Judy had planted a few years ago. I wanted to move them so they wouldn't be lost because we will be starting to build a new house in their current location.

These are the hibiscus trees in the field where the house will be built

This is where they were moved to

This is where they were moved to. It was so hot that they almost died when they were transplanted. We had to water them three times a day to get them to root. Finally after a few weeks of lots of watering and fertilizing they started to bloom again.

This is the guava tree behind the row of bushes

This is a guava tree behind the row of bushes. The Hondurans call it a gwayava. There is no fruit on it because as soon as a fruit appears, before it even gets ripe enough, someone walking by will always take it. I tasted one once and I have to admit it was pretty fantastic.

✳ September 22, 2008

Today there are guys who have come to replace some sinks in the bathroom. I assume they are plumbers. They all wear flip flops. There is no such thing as safety footwear although I have seen the watchmen wear rubber boots while cutting the grass from time to time. I guess they are almost the same thing. Peter gives the guy cutting the opening with a loud handsaw a pair of ear plugs and safety glasses so all the wood and tile chips don't fly into their eyes and they say they don't want them. One guy laughs and says "I haven't used safety glasses or ear plugs in 26 years and I am ok. I don't need them." We walk away as they laugh at us and breathe in clouds of dust and continue to use loud equipment. I pick up my dogs to make sure they don't get exposed or hurt. I walk down the hall and realize how crazy that sounds.

This is my little kitchen garden in the flower bed outside the kitchen

✳ September 23, 2008

There are some really amazing things growing on this property. There are three really large mango trees that produce an enormous amount of fruit. There are lime trees, the one guava tree, coconut palms and banana trees. I have started some papaya from seeds I found in a papaya that I was eating. It was so easy to get them to germinate and now I have some trees that are a few inches tall. I will transplant them so that we can have papayas soon. I am trying to germinate some macadamia nuts that I have brought from my recent trip to Hawaii. I would also like to try to see if coffee will grow. I hope I can plant a big garden which could provide lots of food. If I can show the watchmen and their wives how they can grow a few things they can always have some fresh food in their diets instead of just beans, fish and rice.

✳ September 24, 2008

The windows and doors in the house are all mahogany. It is a magnificent wood, very hard and resistant to most termite damage and other bugs that would prefer to literally eat you out of house and home. Every few years this wood needs to be refinished and sealed so that it can be protected against the harsh sun and rain. There is a guy who has provided a verbal quote to Peter to refinish them. Roger has agreed to have the work done. The guy that is doing the job needs to give Peter a written quote and we ask him to bring it by so we can start the work right away. Peter was in La Ceiba when the guy came over with the contract and he will only speak with him. He informs me that he needs a deposit to buy materials and he needs Peter to sign the contract before he will start. He then explains he will begin on Monday if we can sign and get the money. Today is Tuesday and we were hoping he could start tomorrow however, that is how it goes in Honduras. Everything takes its own time and very few business people have any inventory or supplies so partial payment gives them the cash to buy products and hire guys until the job is done and the balance is paid. Most people don't own their own vehicle or have tools so when you hire a tradesman typically you have to go get him and you have to have all the tools and supplies to fix the problem. Plus you have to feed them lunch. They just come and assume you will feed them. We had never heard of such a custom and if someone hadn't explained it to us we wouldn't have figured it out in a million years.

✳ September 25, 2008

It's odd that I cannot determine how old anyone is here. Everyone looks 15-18 years old or they look really old. The person that is anywhere in between is impossible for me to guess. I thought the cleaning lady was maybe 18 years old and she tells me she is 28 years old and has five children. Holy shit! I never would have guessed it. The electrician that works around the house looks like a little kid and he tells me he has two kids of his own and is 27. I really just have no clue. I think about going to the fair as a child at the end of each summer. There was always a guy that stood at a booth and guessed your age. If he gets it wrong you win a prize. That guy would be bankrupt in this town, unless of course it's just me.

✳ September 26, 2008

Its 33 degrees today in the house and I just can't stand to be anywhere other than my bedroom which is a cool 30.2 degrees C.

✳ September 27, 2008

Unfortunately, Marco the translator/assistant had to go! He thought he was more important than everyone else on the team. He felt it was ok to just boss everyone around and avoid doing any work himself. He got very upset if Peter asked him to do anything that was not translating. We are all expected to do anything and everything when necessary to get a job done. When there is no translating to be done he could either be unpaid or if he wanted to continue getting a full day's salary he would be required to do whatever else might be necessary. We all are. He developed an expectation that he was to be picked up and driven home every day. He didn't have his own vehicle and normally Peter would pick him up on the way somewhere but, now that things are getting busier and appointments are coming to the house this is not always possible. Most people that do not have their own car just start walking out to the road when they want to go home. Once on the road to town they try to hitch a ride. He would expect Peter to find him a drive. He also expected to be taken out to lunch every day. There were occasions where they happened to meet people during a lunch so of course he got his lunch provided. He then assumed he would always get fed. In the end after much discussion we all decided he needed to go.

We learned a lot from him and all the things we needed to make crystal clear before we hired anyone else.

Juan is now the guy who is going to help out when we need it. Before he got the job it was clearly defined that when there is nothing to translate then in order to get a salary whatever is required will be asked. Juan is a lot more flexible and we are much clearer about expectations right up front if you want the job this is what might be required. We tell him to bring his lunch and if we can drop you off and pick you up we will try. If not then you need to find a way home. Get a bicycle, call a friend, walk, whatever you need to do to get home. This makes it clear and avoids some of the problems we in advertently caused with Marco.

Marco was a man that really wanted to work with his church. His thing was working with children and this job was not the right fit for him or us. He couldn't see that this was a way to make a bit of money in order to have the ability to do what he really wanted to do later. We feel bad that it didn't work out but, shit happens.

Juan is hopefully a better fit. After his first day on the job things seem to be going well.

On the drive back to town, we notice two young girls waiting for the bus on the road. Peter asks them if they want a ride to town and they say yes and jump in. It is a long, dirty, dusty walk at this time of year and when we have room, a lift is always offered. The drive takes maybe 8 minutes and within those short 8 minutes Juan is in love with Lisia. He has her telephone number and they have made a date for coffee. Now that's smooth!

They need a good cafe in this town (not to mention a bakery and a real butcher shop). Where do people go for a coffee, I wonder? Where I come from, there is a coffee shop on all four corners of some streets.

✳ September 28, 2008

There is a flurry of activity around the house today. A plumber is here to replace a toilet. The guy that is refinishing the wood has finally come back to get the contract signed and now he has decided he wants more money as a deposit. He wants 50% of the money up front for the job.

The watchmen have chopped down a coconut tree that was just outside the kitchen window. I am so sad to see it go but they say it is dying and they will plant a new one in its place. I watch two of them cut down the coconut tree with machetes and a rope. Holy shit, I can't believe how they quickly hack it down by hand. After the tree comes down, I look out the window and I see them all eating something. I go out and ask them what they are eating? They show me this large white thing that looks like a femur (the large bone in your leg). They say it is the core of the palm that is located near the top of the tree. When they say it in Spanish "Corazon de Palma", it immediately hits me... The direct translation is "heart of the palm". Oh my God! I cannot believe this is a fresh "heart of palm". We get them back in Canada in cans. I have only ever had them in tiny pieces. I have eaten them in salads and it has never even dawned on me to consider what a heart of palm is or that it is literally the heart of a palm tree! They gave me two large pieces to try and it was amazing. To eat it fresh is nothing like the stuff in the can. It is delicious! I ask him how they eat it and he says like this and sticks a piece in his mouth. I ask him if they cook it or eat it with anything else and he says no, just like this. He hands me a large piece and I am so excited to figure out how to eat it the best way.

Tonight I am going to make a salad with the fresh heart of palm. I have to really dig on the internet to find out what to do with it. There are not a ton of recipes for fresh hearts of palm. I discover you can eat it raw or you can cook it. I make a salad with the heart raw and then I decide to boil it gently until it is tender and immediately put it in vinaigrette while it is still warm, much like a German potato salad. This way it will absorb all the flavours as it cools and eventually chills to make a nice cool salad. I create a vinaigrette with some red wine vinegar, some olive oil, grated onion, garlic, some fresh parsley and basil from my herb garden and some spices like hot chili flakes, salt, pepper, Italian seasonings and lime juice.

It is intoxicatingly, ridiculously good and we all eat as much as we can of this abundance. I go over to give some to Manuel to see if he likes it this way. He thinks it's good or at least that is what he tells me. Who really knows?

This is the fresh heart of palm

This is the fresh heart of palm. It was a least 1 foot long. I was so excited to get this amazing gift and even more excited about what to do with it.

✳ September 29, 2008

The power went off again today and of course the generator still doesn't work. There is a problem with the alternator. The electrician is here and he thinks he knows how to fix it. He says he has the part at home that he thinks can repair the problem. So, they jump in the truck and go to his house to get the part.

While they are gone I think of all those people in town who don't even have power at all. They have a fire outside the house that they cook on but, for me to even imagine no coffee maker, no stove, no fridge, no fans, and no lights to read at night. Just imagine it.

I have a new white toilet in my bathroom. Why is that such a good thing? It is so you can see any mosquitoes should they be waiting to bite you on the bum. Don't laugh! They bite more than just bums and you don't want a bite there whether you are a boy or a girl!

✳ September 30, 2008

We have determined that the reason the stove doesn't work so well is because there is a kink in the propane line that feeds into the house. All this time we have only been getting a small amount of propane coming through, and that's why the stove never gets hot enough. We need to get some new replacement tubing for the line and we have to call a guy who can fix it. It's a beautiful new gas stove and it has always been so bizarre that the stove never got hot enough. There were times when we would create barriers around the one burner so no breeze could interfere with the flame. We would always have to turn off any ceiling fans that were near to the stove. It was a comedy to try to get water to boil. After 20 minutes we usually just ended up putting in the pasta and hoped it would soften in the warm water enough to cook it. We could never get meat or chicken to brown or potatoes to fry even if you stood there for an hour. Trust me I did it!

So, we have to order the part to fix the propane line; and then go get the guy and bring him to the house; and give him all the tools and get him to fix it; pay him and then take him home.

The next door neighbor came over this afternoon and she left some fresh salsa in the fridge. I was in the bedroom and the house is so big if someone is yelling at the door you can't always hear it. She thought I might be having a nap and didn't want to come down to my room, so she just put it in the fridge. What a nice surprise!

Maybe I will make chicken enchiladas tonight to go with the salsa.

Spicy: adjective
Piquant, zesty. a spicy tomato salsa
High spirited, lively.
Slightly scandalous, risqué. a spicy romantic affair

❋ October 1, 2008

We got the funniest phone call today. It was a call from the guy who did our dry cleaning back in Canada. His store is located in the grocery store in our old home town. Can you even imagine? Out of the blue, a call from the dry cleaner! I later found out my mother-in-law gave him our number. He wanted to hear our voices and said he missed us. I told him I miss him more now that I have to iron all of Peter's shirts! He said he wanted us to come and visit and I told him sure no problem. I will be sure to bring my laundry with me too!

❋ October 2, 2008

One of the guys that works around the property was staring at my little garden outside the kitchen. He asks me lots of questions about what I have planted and when I explain that it is a little herb garden and it is perfectly located outside the kitchen so that when I need something for cooking I just go outside and get what I need. He is fascinated about herbs and had no idea there were so many or that you would plant a garden just for the purposes of cooking. He thinks this is so unusual. He is also the same guy that is fascinated by my salt grinder. He just thinks it's amazing that you can buy chunks of salt and grind them as you use the salt. He is dazzled by the engineering of the grinder and is amazed they make such things.

Today is 36.5 degrees C. Holy shit, is it hot! We have not had rain in weeks and everything is so dry and dusty. I have a million bites on me and even Lulu has bites and red legs from the rough grass. The grass is so rough I think it scratches her or she is allergic to it. The bottom side of her feet are red and she constantly licks them. We are all itchy and scratchy!

It's funny how the people in Honduras say Yamaha. Or it's funny how we say it! We say YA-MA-HA and they say YAMA-HA. I think it's because in Spanish there is only one accent in a word and typically it's the pen-ultimate one. So they made a Japanese word fit into the Spanish format. Interesting don't you think?

❄ October 3, 2008

This morning I found 2 dead chicks on the deck near the pool. These are the yellow tailed Orioles that sound like they are saying "eat-yer-meat". They had a nest under the roof tiles on the pool side of the house. It's so sad because the babies were quite large in size already but, I am convinced they committed suicide and jumped to their deaths because it was just too damn hot under that roof.

I transplanted some small plants today. They were flowers for my border around the driveway. I planted them after the hottest part of the day and 2 hours after I planted them they were almost dead in spite of a good watering and being shielded from the direct sun. That heat is truly unbelievable. I watered them all again and separated each leaf to give the whole plant lots of air and to see if I could save them. As nightfall came it was still hot however, without the beating sun on them they seemed to perk up.

❄ October 4, 2008

Wow, today it's 38 degrees C. I watered all the plants and shrubs every 2 hours to keep them going. It hasn't rained in weeks and I wonder if this is why people don't grow things here. There is too much effort required to keep them alive during the extreme heat.

Miraculously my baby plants have survived the first day of being transplanted. By 9:30 am of day two I question whether they will make it another day. I will put up some patio umbrellas and palm fronds to shield the new plants from the extreme heat of the day. I have already watered twice by 9:30 am and even the hearty hibiscus plants we transplanted last week are still struggling. I have given them as much black soil I can find and some Miracle Grow to see if I can help them along until they are rooted well. What a harsh environment! I think I will be watering a few more times today.

It's very odd that I drink a lot of water but hardly ever have to pee. I guess I sweat most of it out.

I saw Manuel's wife today. (I am embarrassed to say I don't know her name.) She is fishing on the side of the river that runs at the front of the house near the driveway. I see her fishing almost every day. She stands on the bank or on the bridge with a piece of wood and some fishing line wrapped around it with a hook and a small weight on the end. She catches tilapia from the brackish water and she then hands them to her younger daughter Maria who cleans them. I have heard there is a 7 foot crocodile that lives in the river although I have never seen it.

✳ October 5, 2008

Peter was driving down to Trujillo today when he saw 2 horses on the side of the road. He sensed something was wrong when one of the horses was trying to nudge the other to move. He said the horse was clearly stressed. He pulled over and noticed that one of the horses was stuck in the barbed wire fencing that is everywhere. There was a bit of wire that the horse was caught in and just could not get free. Peter got out a pair of cutters and clipped the wire which instantly freed the horse. It was also fortunate that the horse had not hurt itself. The two horses just calmly trotted off on their way. Sometimes the smallest thing makes a world of difference. I always remember the quote that says "no act of kindness, no matter how small is ever wasted". Especially by the recipient of that kindness!

✳ October 6, 2008

Today the weather has cooled off a bit. I never thought I would say it cooled off to 35 degrees before.

Peter built me a little structure around my struggling plants. I can take some dead palm fronds and place them on the wooden frame which is over the young plants. They are shielded from the sun and the fronds will not squash the plants or fall over. Perfect!

✳ October 7, 2008

It rained last night for a few minutes. I am glad I had my support structure and my palm leaves over the little plants because when it rains here, it RAINS HARD and heavy. My little plants that were under the structure seem to be ok but my other little basil plants in the kitchen flowerbed have taken a beating. You have to be tough to live in this place, be you man or plant!

Oh my God! We had steak and lobster tonight. Roger brought an entire beef tenderloin with him from Canada in his luggage. He brings meat and cheese in vacuum sealed packages and surprisingly they don't give him any problems at the airport. I made a nice chimichurri sauce with my own grown herbs. We grilled the steaks and had lobsters with garlic butter. I was in total heaven. There were no words to describe my happiness and how satisfied and fulfilled I felt. Yum!

❋ October 8, 2008

I clipped the watchmen's dogs' nails today. I am so glad they feel safe enough with me to allow me to do this strange thing. I clipped their very, very long nails. I also cleaned out their ears with ear cleaner and q-tips and I gave them a good brushing. The guards stare at me and are just fascinated at what I am doing. They shake their heads in amazement. The dogs loved the brushing and even tolerated me cleaning their ears and trimming their nails. I think they just like anyone touching them and being nice to them.

I told you how the flies around here grow to joke shop sizes. Today I saw the biggest fly I have ever seen. It was as big as my whole thumb... Like 2 inches. Can you imagine seeing a giant fly? I was utterly fascinated and repulsed at the same time. Creepy and disgusting!

❋ October 9, 2008

Last night Roger shared the most amazing sight with Peter. They went out for a swim in the ocean and when you walk out you stir up the plankton that is on the bottom. When the plankton gets stirred up it lights up. It looks like there are diamonds sparkling in the water. Roger joked about how you would be all messed up if you were on drugs seeing it for the first time. It was like magic and when they walked out of the water and back onto the beach, all the diamonds fell off them and back into the water. Nature is truly amazing.

Today it feels like this is a large plantation with so many people here. There are lots of people doing all kinds of jobs. There are eight guys refinishing windows. They do all of it by hand with sandpaper on blocks of wood and scrapers. There are people fixing a boat. There are people clearing and organizing all the bits and pieces in the bodega (the garage/shop). You always need some weird thing down here and you cannot always get exactly what you are looking for, so you never throw anything away. You keep things for their parts and usually find a need for them. It's like an episode of practical, organized hoarders. The watchmen are all clearing the driveways and making sure cars and vehicles are clean. I was laughing to myself because the watchmen were wearing rubber boots instead of flip flops;

and they are wearing the ear plugs and the safety glasses that Peter gave them, which they insisted previously that they did not need. I was also busy transplanting some oyster plants along the outside wall of the west wing of the house. There is full production going on and we are all working to make the property look its best.

✳ October 10, 2008

I made a pizza last night and now I am convinced a wood fired oven outside would be awesome. You could make great pizza, roasted meat and fish and fresh bread. You could make enough bread for yourself and the other families. Another great benefit would be to have an oven located out of the house so it wouldn't heat up the house.

Roger said that he wants to start planting more trees on the property. I am suggesting he plants Eureka lemons (like the kind you buy in stores in North America), limes, grapefruit and mangos for my own selfish reasons. He then made me very happy when he said he wanted to get some donkeys. I have an absolute love affair going with donkeys. I just think they are so lovely and people are always so mean to them all over the world. I would love to have some well adjusted happy donkeys. I brought books with me on raising donkeys and so I told him he needs at least 2 of them because they cannot be alone. I am very excited about this news.

✳ October 11, 2008

We had to cut down an old mango tree today where the new house is going to be built. We cleared all the hibiscus bushes and now the mango tree needs to go. It was so sad because it is an old tree abundant with fruit. Mangos grow so easily and with virtually no intervention from man. So, we shall plant another one somewhere else and hopefully it will be healthier than this one was.

I saw one of the dogs today out on the back lawn near the beach. He was eating the inside of a green coconut like a dog would be chewing on a Kong toy in Canada. It was amazing to watch how he got all the meat out.

I found a frog on the book shelf in my bedroom. What is his story and how did he get here? I picked him up and put him outside where I hope he will be very happy and not be eaten by anything.

✳ October 12, 2008

Hurricane Gustav is making trouble for me today. When a storm is approaching you can always tell because the sea is very violent first thing in the morning. The waves are big and noisy where they are typically just quietly lapping up the shore.

Normally I don't really care and can stay at the house. Today however, I am to be a part of a delegation of people that are going to a nearby Garifuna village to see a presentation of their proposed cultural centre.

Nine of us took a small boat along the Caribbean shoreline until we arrived at some remote lagoons. Hurricane Gustav happened to be pounding Cuba at that moment and causing some pretty nasty waves for our journey as well. I am not a fan of boats. I wouldn't get in a boat like this on a clear day but, I was obligated to go so, go I did. The boat was crashing up and down, up and down, pounding us like we were on a roller coaster ride. I was very relieved when we reached the lagoons because the waters were instantly calmer. These lagoons are a combination of both salt and fresh water and are full of mangroves. Mangroves are trees that grow with all their gnarly roots showing above the water. Mangroves are very important environmentally because they provide a natural sheltering belt against storms, flooding and coastal erosion. They also provide a dynamic ecosystem for plants and animals that have adapted to this tropical inter-tidal zone. That sounds logical however what it basically means is that the mangroves provide a nice swampy area for creatures like snakes, gigantic spiders, crocodiles, fish, crustaceans, monkeys and a whole lot of creepy crawly things.

We drove through one mangrove forest and of course there are plenty of hungry mosquitoes happy to greet you. We drive through and under all the branches and roots. At times we all needed to lie down flat in the boat to get through the lower roots. One of the other women in the boat was smart enough to bring a can of "OFF" with her. She could have sold it to each of us for $50 a spray and we would have paid it. I certainly would have. I can't imagine how the driver knows where we are going because it looks like we are in a maze. We finally arrive at a river bank in the middle of nowhere and I swear if we didn't have that guide we never ever would have found it. We tie up the boat and walk for a few minutes until we reach a clearing and then a road. Cars are waiting for us at this point and we divide up to fit into the vehicles. The cars take us to the location of the proposed site.

The local people are all excited to see us coming. Basically we hope that this village can help to encourage tourism in the area. This cultural centre will be of interest to tourists. If they are coming on a vacation or a stop on a cruise they will want to see local attractions. The Garifuna people hope this cultural centre will provide a way to sustain their culture and community and provide income to support their people.

They do a presentation for us and tell us of their history and how they came from all parts of the Caribbean. They showed us how they made certain specialities like Cassava bread and how they can also turn Cassava into a drink. Cassava is a starchy root vegetable sometimes called Yucca that is often cooked like a potato and if dried it is used in some countries to form Tapioca. They bring out some traditional food and they show us their dancing like the traditional Punta dance. The event was started with a spiritual prayer that was in the form of song and everyone formed a circle and held hands while the key members lead the prayer. They spoke of keeping their distinct culture alive and the things they need to do to protect their land from being sold and separated. It was really quite an impressive presentation and we had a great time.

We travelled back through the maze of the mangroves. Once again ducking and lying down in the boat when necessary to get through the low branches and roots. The driver was only too happy to inform us that Anacondas live in these mangroves. I was quite relieved to say we did not meet any on this particular day. There were no shortages of giant, nasty looking spiders in their elaborate mammoth webs. I also cannot forget to mention my favorite friends - the mosquitoes. There were plenty of them around to greet us and we could hear lots of monkeys in the distance but, we never actually saw any of them.

We emerged from the lagoons and had to go way out into the ocean back along the shoreline to Trujillo. We were protected in the mangroves and you couldn't tell that the ocean had become quite a bit more violent with huge swells and massive choppy waves as the day progressed. The storm was getting worse and we just might be getting a full blown hurricane in a few hours. The ride was extremely choppy and all I could think of was if the boat tipped over could I swim to shore? We were quite a distance out however, the shore was visible and I liked to imagine that I was enough of a good swimmer to make it should I be tested. Within a few minutes of being in open waters we were all completely soaking wet, right down to our underwear. It was as if we jumped in the ocean. There was so much salt on my face that I couldn't even wipe it out of my eyes because I had nothing dry to wipe them with. For most of the trip I had my eyes closed so the salt would not constantly sting and burn.

We approached the dock we left from, which is really more of a long cement pier. We all needed to try to hold the boat steady in order for one person at a time to get out. It was truly a balancing act and you had to make several attempts of timing the waves perfectly before finally being able to get out. People fell back and tried again and again to finally manage to get off. It was extremely rough at this point but, I was happy that we were at least at the shore and not out in the ocean. In the end the waves were too rough for all of us to get off on the pier and the driver just let the boat drift towards the beach in order for the last few to get out. I just jumped off the boat and walked up the beach to Rogues. I needed a cocktail!

I told you I don't like boats and I will never go out when it's rough like that again. I got to the restaurant completely soaking wet and remarkably I was able to keep my phone dry because I always keep it in a Ziploc bag (because you just never know!) I called Peter and told him I was sitting there until I dried out and if he wanted to join me for a beer I was celebrating being alive!

✳ October 13, 2008

I heard that Stella who lives down the road has a baby leopard or a jaguar. They are not sure what it is. She said the mother was killed and someone rescued the baby and gave it to her. You never really know around here. Sometimes people kill the mother in order to steal and sell the baby. Poverty makes people do desperate things. It is a huge problem and although it is illegal to traffic in these babies it does happen. I am dying to go see it. When would you ever have the chance to see a baby like that up close?

My brugmansias are coming up. They are sometimes called angel's trumpets or daturas. These plants can grow to become a large tree that has huge white bell shaped flowers. They open at night and have an incredible scent. I always grow them at home in Canada and to start them from seed or propagation is very easy. The nice thing is they will not have to be taken in for the winter like they do in Canada. It's very exciting to imagine how big they can get here.

There is a perfectly shaped mango tree near the driveway just past the front gate. It is so large and has such a perfect shape to it. I just think it is such a magnificent tree. I think it should be the logo when they create the farm as part of the development. Maybe we can call it Mango Tree Farm or Mango Tree Acres?

✳ October 14, 2008

Juan was at the house today. He asked me if he could use the microwave to make his Cup-O-Noodles. I got the electric kettle out and filled it with water and then plugged it in. When the water came to a boil, I filled the Styrofoam cup that the noodles come in. I explained that it is better if he boils the water separately, either with a kettle or in a mug in the microwave, and then adds the boiling water to the Cup-O-Noodles in the Styrofoam. I know that this is not the healthiest lunch in the world however you don't need to add the Styrofoam issue to the problem as well. He was totally surprised and had no idea. Most people do not have microwaves in their homes. Many people do go to the big chain gas stations because they all have microwaves and many people go to buy the soup and prepare it right there in the gas station. They line up for them. It's like when TV dinners came out and everyone couldn't get enough of them. It was so modern! I have to admit if you are stranded with a flat tire (and they happen a lot) a Cup-O-Noodles in a gas station can be a very good thing. I know it firsthand.

After the water boiled he couldn't stop staring at the electric kettle. He had never seen one before. Once again the things you take for granted that can be completely unheard of in another part of the world.

I was walking down the long driveway this evening and I noticed the large rocks of granite and marble and slate. I know these stones come from nature however, isn't it amazing how you never think it's possible that they could be under your feet on a driveway. Now if I could just slice them and glue them together to make a slab for my kitchen, wouldn't that be a craft project?

✳ October 15, 2008

Friday is Carly's birthday. I will make her an apple crisp – she wanted that instead of a birthday cake.

Today I noticed something cute. I have always left a large bowl filled with clean water in the car port for the watchmen's dogs. The dogs don't have clear, clean water. They just drink out of the cloudy brackish river. I know the guards never even think about it. Rather than try to get them to change their ways, I just put some water out and change it daily and the dogs have been drinking from it. Manuel has noticed this and today I saw that he had a bowl of water out at the front of his house for his dogs. I have also noticed the dogs around the property have started to look better. They are not as skinny and their coats are starting to look a bit better. I have been giving them dog food daily for the last 2 months. I have also been giving them all our food scraps from our meals since we have arrived. I always give the food to their owners so they can feed their dogs. I really think there is starting to be an improvement and they seem to be a bit more playful.

✳ October 16, 2008

We removed some really large ticks from the dogs' ears and I gave two of the watchmen a set of tweezers to remove them going forward. Yesterday we noticed Tigra scratching her ear and crying. I knew she was clearly stressed so Manuel helped me by holding her and I removed a huge engorged tick. It is such a small thing that can simply torture a poor animal. A pair of tweezers and someone showing how to help the animal is such a small thing. But, if you don't even know what tweezers are or that something simple can help your animal in pain, it can really be a huge deal.

Every once in a while we get someone who gives us grapefruit or oranges. The funny thing is they always look unripe just like my green juice in San Pedro Sula. They are usually green on the outside and the inside because they need cooler nights in order to turn yellow or orange. We don't have cooler nights in the summer so they stay green. The taste is great. They are delicious in flavor, just odd in appearance. I wonder if we can get some seeds for pink grapefruit?

There is a huacal tree near the lime tree in the front yard. It is also called a calabash tree and it produces a weird looking fruit that is like a gourd. The fruit can grow on any part of the tree including the trunk. The locals pronounce it WA-KAL and it looks like a large shiny avocado. I asked Manuel what it was and he made me walk up to the tree and feel the fruit. They are very hard and he explained that it is not something you eat. He said when it is ready it will fall off the tree. They take it and saw off the top because it is as hard as a coconut. They would either pick out the inside or just leave it in the sun to dry out and then they can easily remove the interior. He explained that many poor people in Honduras use these as cups and bowls or to carry water because they can't afford dishes.

This is what the huacal tree looks like. Notice that the fruit grows from the branches or the trunk.

This is the huacal fruit close up

✳ October 17, 2008

We went to a bar on the beach called The Delphin (The Dolphin) and we watched the Honduras vs. Canada qualifying game for FIFA 2010. It was lots of fun. I happen to really love watching international soccer. It was fun to dress up in our Canadian T-shirts and place small bets on the game and then yell back and forth with the locals who were supporting the Honduran team. The town went crazy when Honduras won 2-1. We had to drive back through town on the drive of shame. We had our Canadian flags on our trucks and the whole community was chanting "HON-DU-RAS!" as we drove by. We celebrated their victory and con-gratulated their win. It was all in good fun and we had a great time.

Did you know that a large bullfrog in Honduras can shit the same size as a small dog? I would come out to the back deck around the pool in the morning and find massive turds and wonder what the hell they were from. Roger told me they were from frogs. Holy shit! The stuff you see in Honduras!

This morning I finally went over to see the baby jaguar. He is very little and doesn't look like a jaguar to me. It's so sad that he is currently in a parrot cage but, he is very sweet and they call him Yuma. When most people come near him he hisses in fear because he has lost his mother and he is just a baby. Stella's daughter is taking care of him. When she comes near him he is fine and she puts her hand in the cage and he lets her pet him. As she is rubbing his head he falls asleep in her hands on his little perch. I come near him and speak softly and he also let me pet him and once again he falls asleep.

My heart literally breaks for him and I wish I could build him a larger cage. Stella has many animals on her property. There are lots of parrots, dogs, horses, cows and now this little baby jaguar. I wonder if he can be raised enough so he can be released but, I don't know if that is the intention. They explained that he is eating and sleeping and pooping, so this is all a good indication of his health. After I get home and do some digging on the internet I discover he is probably an ocelot not a jaguar. They are endangered and they are called tigrillo in Honduras. They are mostly nocturnal and sleep in trees. I don't feel so bad now that he is sleeping on a perch. I wonder what they are feeding him and does he need milk?

Yuma the baby ocelot

On the drive back to the house I saw a mother donkey and a fuzzy baby donkey walking along beside her. They are in the lot right outside our front gate. I pull over on the quad and I happen to have some bird seed with me. I bring seeds as a treat for the parrots when I go to Stella's. They normally get fruit but not seeds so it's a change for them. I hold out my hand and surprisingly the mother comes right up to me and eats the seeds out of my hand. They both let me touch them and give them a little scratch. They were so beautiful. This is so what I live for. I am grateful for meeting them and I happily go on my way.

I came back to the house and told Roger about my exciting interactions with the donkeys outside the front gate. He told me to go see if I could encourage them to come in the gate and on to the property. Right now they just wander up and down along the main road into town. They could easily get hurt by all the cars going by and certainly they would have more food on the property as well as more protection. I was so excited. I went back out and opened the gate and tried to entice them with more bird seed but, they were not interested in coming in and so they just calmly wandered away. I said good bye and they were gone as they came. It was a precious moment in time and I am still glad I met them. They were just interested in doing their own thing. I can't blame them for that.

 October 19, 2008

Scorching: adjective
Very hot
Harsh, severe (as in criticism)

It was 38.7 degrees C in the shade today and 75% humidity. Whoa that's a hot one!

Today I made a feast. I made some flatbreads, a hot artichoke dip as well as a lime chick pea dip. We had grilled steaks, chicken, baked potatoes, a tossed salad and for dessert, another banana cake.

Lime Garlic Chick Pea Dip

1 can chick peas/garbanzos drained/rinsed

1 clove garlic – crushed

1 lime – juiced

4-5 sprigs fresh thyme

Hot sauce – to taste

¼ cup olive oil

2 sun dried tomatoes in oil – chopped fine

1 tbsp. fresh parsley/cilantro

Salt/pepper

- In a food processor add chick peas and all other ingredients. Process until it makes a thick dip. Taste it and if you like more lime or salt, add it. If it is too thick you can always add a bit of water.

Banana Cake

3 ¼ cups flour

3 ½ tsp. of baking powder (I had no baking powder so I used 2 tsp. baking soda & ½ tsp. salt)

½ tsp. cinnamon (ground)

4 eggs

2 ½ cups sugar

1 cup olive oil

¼ cup milk

3 cups mashed bananas

2 tsps. rum (or vanilla)

1 1/3 cups walnuts or walnuts and shredded coconut.

- Heat the oven to 350 degrees F. Butter and flour large glass Pyrex dish (3QT) or 2 loaf pans.

- Sift dry ingredients: flour, baking powder, cinnamon.

- Beat eggs and sugar until thick with an electric mixer. Approximately 4 minutes.

- Add oil, then bananas, milk and rum. Then mix in the dry ingredients by hand being careful not to over mix and finally mix in walnuts.

- Pour into pan(s).

- Bake in a 350 degree F oven for 1 hour to 1 ½ for the large pan less if it is in two pans. You want the top nicely browned and when you insert a toothpick in the centre of the cake it comes out clean.

- Top with some powdered sugar.

Hot Artichoke Dip

1 can of artichoke hearts – drained

¼ cup mayonnaise

1 tbsp. lime juice

1 tbsp. mustard

1 clove garlic (crushed)

1 tsp. Worcestershire

1 cup grated cheddar

4 spring onions – chopped finely

1 cup grated Parmesan

1 large onion – sliced fine and caramelized (fry on low for approximately 30 minutes with olive oil and touch of balsamic vinegar)

Hot sauce – as much as you like

1 tsp. onion powder

1 tsp. fresh chopped basil

1 tsp. fresh thyme

1 tsp. fresh cilantro or parsley

- In a medium sized bowl chop the artichokes as fine as you can and add all the other ingredients. Taste it and add more lime or hot sauce. It should be a thick mix. Put into a baking dish and top with more cheese. Bake at 350 degrees F until hot and bubbling, approximately 20 minutes. Serve with bread or crackers.

☀ October 20, 2008

I have been to some local restaurants where they fill Ziploc bags full of water and leave them on the tables to keep the flies away. They say it messes with the lenses of their eyes so they won't land near it. It does seem to work. How did someone figure that out?

☀ October 23, 2008

I went to Miami for 3 days. If you are not a resident of Honduras you must leave every 90 days and then you can come back. I am sure it's just so they can charge you the 644 lempira ($30 US) international fee, to leave the country. I was thrilled to leave for a few days. I went to a nice hotel. I got my hair coloured. Sorry but, I just cannot imagine getting my hair done in Honduras. No one even has blond hair here unless they color it themselves with a box of dye they buy in the US and I am just not there yet.

I was so excited to eat all the things I can't get in Trujillo. I met Carly and we stayed at the JW Marriott hotel right in the business district. We walked around the streets for a while and found a great restaurant. I really enjoyed my steak with spinach. (I can't believe how much I crave spinach!) I also had asparagus and yellow peppers. It was divine. I started off my meal with an arugula salad with walnuts and blue cheese. Oh my God, it was all so good!

Carly is a Marriott gold member so we got to stay on the presidential floor. They had a complimentary lounge where you could have free breakfast, appetizers and cocktails. In the evening they serve warm cookies before bed. They had all the English newspapers and CNN was on the TV in English! It was all so decadent and I just loved it. The best part was turning on the air conditioning until the room was freezing cold and climbing under the duvet because I was TOO COLD! I haven't been too cold in months.

It was so relaxing to walk along the water, go to shopping malls and buy a smoothie. Something so trivial and small can remind me of home. I have to admit after 2 days I was missing my husband and my dogs and I was ready to go back. I found all kinds of silly things to buy and bring back with me. I also discovered a scale in the room and I was shocked to see that I had lost 20 pounds. I knew my clothes were getting looser and I thought I had lost maybe 5-10 pounds but, 20 was a pleasant surprise. Mark that down as a good thing about living in Honduras.

When I was on the airplane coming back to Honduras, they gave me a normal customs form like you get entering any country. On this form they ask you some very weird questions. I am not sure if they have an issue with some odd translations or what but, I don't understand what they are asking.

They ask "what is the country of procedure?" What does that mean? There is a woman sitting next to me that is from Honduras and speaks English, so I ask her if she can tell me what this is. She says "what is the country you departed from?" Who the hell would understand that from those words?

Here is another one that makes no sense to me: "Have you enjoyed in the last 6 months exoneration tributes?" What the hell is that? She explains that if you are Honduran you get to declare $1000 duty free for things purchased in the last 6 months and they want to know if you have used it. I am sure it must make sense in Spanish. Honestly, and this is on their customs form.

✳ October 24, 2008

Manuel's dog Solita had puppies last night. There are 6 of them. Two are tanned color like her and the others are black like the father. She had them under a big cement platform beside Manuel's house. I went over to see them all. Solita was so happy to see me and was as gentle as ever. She didn't get concerned when I was near her babies. I even picked some of them up with no stress to mom. Manuel moved them all. He had an overturned metal boat and he moved them all under the boat. He had a piece of old carpet and some foam that he gave to her to make her comfortable, but essentially they were all just on the sand. I think it was so kind of him to find something he could to make her comfortable. Most people just wouldn't even concern themselves about this kind of an issue at all. I had an extra dog bed and so I washed it and brought it over for her to have a clean place to lie on with her pups. I think they were really surprised to see this nice big bed all freshly cleaned for a dog. I am pretty sure you wouldn't sell many dog beds in this town. Manuel's wife told me how last time the dog had puppies the crocodile that lives in the river ate 2 of them. I can imagine a ton of things to keep them safe, like a fence, or a little shed, even the cement platform seems safer to me. He puts them under a metal boat right beside the river to keep the rain off and I hope for the best. I have to remember that everyone is just doing the best they can, with the resources they have

✳ October 25, 2008

I went back to see the puppies. They were all there under the boat but they were lying on the old carpet and foam and the dog bed was nowhere to be found. I don't ask but, I am pretty sure they took it in the house and the baby is sleeping on it or maybe even little Manuelito. They don't have a crib. The baby is usually sleeping in a hammock during the day but, I guess he sleeps with his mother at night. I am happy that the baby would have someplace to sleep. If you had a baby that needed a bed then the dog shouldn't have a bed that was better but, my heart just breaks for Solita and those puppies. I have to find another bed for Solita. I just hate that they are getting sand all over themselves and they are so exposed. They could so easily roll down and into the water at this stage in their lives.

I made pesto today with my big batch of basil. I am so glad I brought some pine nuts from Canada. It seems like such a luxury. The pesto on pasta made a perfect lunch.

❋ October 26, 2008

Insecticide: Noun
A substance or preparation for killing pests.
The act of killing insects

Today I decided to spray the orange trees that are located right outside the front gate. They are full of black sooty mould. I have had lemon trees before which I assume are very similar. I know how the lemon trees always attract every bug to them because of the sweetness in their leaves and you are constantly battling them. I had some dormant oil in my gardening kit. Dormant oil and sulphur is a mix that you spray on fruit trees first thing in the spring to kill off overwintering bugs. I figure it can't hurt and if I can give them a bit of fertilizer and a bit of TLC they might do very well. They have survived on no attention whatsoever up to this point. I go out the front with the hose and my sprayer and the guards just wonder what the hell I am doing. If it doesn't grow without any help at all, it doesn't grow around here. The trees are lovely mature trees and I am sure they will bear good fruit.

I was sorting my packages of seeds today. The cleaning lady stopped her work to see what I was doing. She didn't know what most of the seeds were. She had never seen asparagus, or red peppers or honeydew melon.

❋ October 27, 2008

I always take Lulu with me and she even comes with me on the quad. I put her in between my legs on the seat. You should just see people looking at me and pointing and laughing because they have never seen anything like it. Lulu is perfectly cute and comfortable. She thinks nothing of being on the seat.

I made a Texas style chili today with my frozen beef tenderloin. It was perfectly spicy and smoky. Texas chili is usually made with no beans. It's all meat and spices.

Beef Chili

You will need:

2 lbs. beef cut into small cubes (use a chuck roast or stewing beef)

1 large onion - chopped finely

3 cloves garlic – chopped finely

1-2 jalapeno peppers

1 green pepper - chopped finely

½ can or approximately 3 tbsp. tomato paste

1 large can tomatoes or tomato puree (I usually drain liquid and add it only if necessary)

1 bottle of beer

1 tsp. granulated garlic

1 tsp. granulated onion

2 tsp. ground coriander

1 tsp. dry oregano

1 tsp. hot paprika

1 tbsp. cumin

½ tsp. cayenne pepper

1 tbsp. chili powder

1 chipotle chili in adobo sauce

1 tsp. salt

1 tsp. pepper

Olive oil

Another difference is that you typically use chunks of meat instead of ground beef. Mine does use tomatoes, so I have decided it is Honduran Chili in the Texas style.

- In a large pan sauté onions, the jalapenos and green pepper in a few tablespoons of olive oil. You could also fry a few slices of bacon and use the fat to fry the vegetables. Cook until the onions are translucent and just starting to brown. Add meat and garlic. Sauté until water evaporates from meat and it starts to brown. Add beer and scrape off all the browned bits on the bottom of pan. Cook 3-4 minutes then add tomato paste and tomatoes along with all spices and seasonings.

- Continue to cook on medium low for 1 -1 ½ hours. If the chili gets too thick, add the reserved tomato liquid or water. Meat should be tender and sauce reduced.

- Serve with grated cheddar cheese, sour cream (or crema if you are in Honduras), chopped onions, chopped cilantro and a squeeze of lime. Don't forget some nice bread. I had to make my own *'cause there ain't no bakery* in my town.

Oh what I would do to have a nice pizza oven!!

✳ October 28, 2008

I made a dog bed today for Solita out of 3 boxes and lots of packing tape. I wanted to make it so she is comfortable and so her puppies can stay contained until they are able to get out of it. However, you can't make it so good that Manuel's family wants to use it in the house. I made a pillow out of two dog blankets I had and some stuffing to make it soft and padded. I hope it's not too nice that they take it away from her. If her pups are contained it can keep them sort of clean and this way they will not constantly have sand in their eyes and mouths. Poor babies!

I went over to give them my dog bed and there below the boat was the first bed I gave them. I think they saw me coming and just put the bed there for my benefit because the dogs were all crowded around the dirty old carpet and foam again. I wiped all the puppies' eyes and mouths of sand and placed them in the clean box. Solita went in with them and I left. Now hopefully they can give the original bed back to Manuelito or the baby to sleep on and Solita can still be comfortable.

✳ October 29, 2008

The river behind the house is really stinky today. It is blocked at the mouth because there has been no rain lately. The river is just stinky stagnant water that has a nice 7 foot crocodile in it. I went up on the bridge and I actually saw the crocodile for the first time. Yup, it's there and it is a decent size! No need for me to go for a swim in the river! Not that I would anyway.

Carly met Dean Martin today on the beach. Peter met an excavator named Elvis Presley! Who would have thought people had those names in Honduras? Funny!

✳ October 30, 2008

Peter decided he was going to install ropes around the top of the bed of the truck so that if there are people in the back they can at least hold on. Everyone thinks he is nuts and no one uses it. Stupid gringo!

I planted radishes 2 days ago and they have already germinated and are starting to grow.

✳ October 31, 2008

Manuel gave me 3 green coconuts today. He went up a small tree and chopped them down for me and then chopped them open on one end. You drink the water from the young coconut and it has a nice mild coconut flavor. The water is high in potassium and is very nourishing. It's great to drink anytime but, if you have had a bit too much alcohol the night before I find it pretty healing if you know what I mean! It's good after working out to replace water and electrolytes too. As the young coconut matures the water diminishes and the flesh becomes thicker. In a young coconut there is lots of water and a small amount of flesh and the flesh is very soft and delicate. How wonderful it is to be in a place where you just go get them from trees in your backyard.

I find the school thing very confusing around here depending on who you talk to. I have been told that kids go to school from grades 1-9 until they are 15 years old. They usually go half days and they call grades 6-9 university. When it rains they don't go. So does this mean they get half the education from a time perspective? And if someone says they have a degree in engineering, is that a real university degree or does that mean they learned it in grade 9?

My lettuce and tomatoes are starting to come up today. Now if I could just get my lavender to germinate and get going I could line the driveway with lavender bushes. They would love the heat. I don't know how much they would like the rainy season though.

Hey, it's Friday night… Date night! And I am making pizza!!

The weeks are just flying by.

✳ November 1, 2008

My moonflowers are starting to come up. I planted them around the little champa or gazebo that is in the back near the pool. They open at night and you are able to see them from the pool.

I made myself a bowl of Red River cereal this morning. It is a flax and cereal mix that you cook like oatmeal. It is a distinctly Canadian hot cereal. I had some left over so I decided to put some in a muffin mix.

Chocolate Chip Breakfast Cereal Muffins

You will need:

1 cup cooked Red River cereal (any cooked breakfast cereal would work)

1 cup brown sugar

1 tsp. orange juice

1 egg

1 cup coconut milk

1 cup instant oats

½ cup instant quinoa

1¼ cups flour

2 tsp. baking soda

1 tsp. salt

½ cup walnuts

½ cup chocolate chips

1 tbsp. olive oil

- In a medium bowl combine wet ingredients. Add cooked cereal, brown sugar, orange juice, egg, oil and coconut milk.

- In another bowl combine all dry ingredients: oats, quinoa, flour, baking soda and salt. Add the wet to the dry ingredients and stir until just combined. Fold in walnuts and chocolate chips. Spoon into muffin cups and bake at 375 degrees F for 20-25 minutes until a toothpick inserted comes out clean.

You could also take this cooked cereal and add it to bread dough. Lesson learned. Never throw away leftover breakfast cereal. You can always use it in muffins or bread.

I decided to get out my dehydrator today and make some dehydrated mango slices for later when the tree has given up all its fruit and we are wishing for mangos. When a plant gives you this abundance of fruit what can you creatively do with all those mangos? I think I will try them in the food dehydrator as well as in the oven to determine which way is better. I also want to try to make some coconut candy which is something I had in Hawaii on the road to Hana. It is a sweet dehydrated coconut that is just like candy. I think it is coconut slices that are dipped in simple syrup and then dried out. Let's give it a try.

The mango tree is a marvel. I just cannot stop being amazed that the tree is so full of fruit. If you stand at the front door you can hear them dropping every few seconds. It is obscene how many mangos you could eat and give away and still have more. What other things can I make?

Fermentation: noun

The chemical breakdown of a substance by bacteria, yeasts or other microorganisms, typically involving effervescence and the giving off of heat.

Involved in the making of beer, wine, vinegar and liquor, in which sugars are converted to ethyl alcohol

Agitation: excitement

Carrie who works on the development with us brought over some mango vinegar that someone made a year ago and gave her to sample. They wouldn't tell her how they made it but they said it only had mangos in it. I went on the internet and found a few ways to make it, so I will try it two ways. One way you take mangos, honey and a bit of water and just let it ferment. The other way is to take some white vinegar and add the fruit to it.

Method 1: Fermenting mangos

Take a large mason jar and remove the top of the lid but keep the ring. Put a piece of fabric around the top so gas can escape and oxygen can enter. Add ¼ cup of honey and fill up the bottle with some cleaned, chopped fruit; you can leave on the skin and leave in the pit. Add water leaving a couple of inches of room at the top. Cover with fabric/cheesecloth and screw on ring to seal and keep bugs out. Leave it for a week; then dump out the fruit when it becomes darkened. After a few days it will ferment like crazy and should smell like yeast. Add more fruit and leave it another week. Ferment for 3-4 weeks stirring occasionally. Once it is complete remove the fruit, seal your vinegar and store in the fridge. The mango vinegar that I tried was over a year old and almost black like balsamic vinegar. You can make this type of fruit scrap vinegar from any fruit.

Or you can take some white vinegar and add fruit to it. Once it browns, discard the fruit. Do this a few times to infuse your vinegar. This vinegar does not need to have the top open as the fruit is just flavoring the vinegar and not fermenting like the first example.

Perhaps I will make mango salsa tonight and serve it on a piece of grilled chicken.

How many things can I make with mangos?

- Mango vinegar
- Dehydrated mango
- Frozen mango slices
- Frozen mango juice ice cubes
- Mango ice cream
- Mango salsa
- Mango juice
- Fresh mango

✳ November 2, 2008

I walked out to the driveway this morning and I found a little tarantula. Now a little tarantula is still a spider that is 3 inches long and fuzzy with big long legs. That's a big spider by my standards! There are plenty bigger than that but, I still don't want it anywhere near me.

I have decided to make some buffalo chicken fingers and French fries. I have hundreds of cook books stored somewhere in the container however, I will have to make due with some ideas from the internet that I will modify with the ingredients that I can get here. I took the chicken and cut it into strips. I coated it in spices and flour and I baked them for a bit with some olive oil. Then I coated them in some breadcrumbs I made with some leftover pan de coco bread. I baked them again with potatoes I had par boiled then coated in olive oil. Once they were toasty brown I coated them in hot sauce, butter and cider vinegar. Pretty darn good, if I do say so myself!

Baked Buffalo Chicken Strips with Oven Fries

You will need:

2 chicken breasts – sliced into long strips

3 tbsp. flour

¼ tsp. salt

¼ tsp. pepper

¼ tsp. cumin

¼ tsp. cayenne pepper

2 baking potatoes – sliced into wedges (or in Honduras any kind of potato!)

1 egg whisked in small bowl

1 cup bread crumbs (you can flavour them or leave them plain)

½ cup hot sauce (Franks if you can get it)

2 tbsp. butter

1 tbsp. cider vinegar

Olive oil

- Step 1: Slice potatoes into chunky wedges. Par boil for 10 minutes or until partially cooked. Remove and let dry and cool.

- Step 2: Slice chicken into even strips. In a medium bowl mix all spices and flour. Toss in chicken slices to coat. Place chicken on a baking sheet with some olive or vegetable oil. Cook in a 375 degree F oven for 5 minutes. Flip and cook for another 5 minutes. Remove from oven then let cool slightly.

- Step 3: Make hot sauce. In a small sauce pan melt butter and remove from heat, add hot sauce and cider vinegar and stir.

- Step 4: Turn up oven to 400 degrees F. Dip chicken strips in egg and coat in breadcrumbs. Place back on baking sheet. Drizzle some olive oil on top of breaded chicken. These are normally fried so you need a bit of oil on the bottom and on top to make these fingers have a similar consistency as a fried chicken strip. Take cooled potato wedges and toss them in olive oil. Place them on the baking sheet with chicken and sprinkle everything with salt and pepper.

- Step 5: Return to oven and bake until the strips are browned and the potatoes are crunchy. You can remove them as they become cooked. I try to keep all the pieces similar sizes so they cook at the same rate. At this final stage both the chicken and the potatoes are cooked when they are just getting crispy. Remove from oven.

- Step 6: Toss the hot chicken strips in the hot sauce, serve with potato wedges and a nice cold beer. If we could get blue cheese I would have also made a dip with carrot and celery sticks.

❋ November 3, 2008

Maybe today I will have Red River cereal with some mangos on top. I think I will go pick about 20 to slice and freeze. Hey, that gives me an idea, what if I make mango, coconut ice cream? I might have to add that one to my list of things to make with mangos.

❋ November 4, 2008

Today I noticed one of the watchmen's dogs acting all weird. This time it is Cheezpa at the front gate. His ear was down and he was acting strangely. I see the dog and in 1 second can tell there is something wrong and he is not even my dog. I approached him and he let me take a look in his ear. There was a tick in his ear the size of a bean! It was the biggest one I have ever seen. There it was huge, engorged and driving the dog nuts. I go back to my room and find another pair of old tweezers. (That's the third pair.) I give them to Manuel and ask Manuel to show Robelio how to take out the tick. Now every watchman has a pair of tweezers and can remove them from their own dogs.

Cheezpa

This is Cheezpa when he is feeling good! I later found out he had 4 ticks in both his ears. Yikes!

✳ November 5, 2008

Last night we watched the US election coverage and Barak Obama won. There are really only two channels that are in English - the Hallmark channel and CNN World. We were facinated to watch the election coverage since we never really watch much of the news. It was really nice to see the Americans feeling happy for the shift in the White House. It was nice to watch a positive man look forward to the future. He has a big mess to clean up and long and bumpy ride ahead of him. For today, it was a day filled with joyful optimism.

Peter was picking up his guys on the way to Guadaloupe to clear some land this morning, when he got pulled over by a policeman standing in the road. The police-man has a cuffed prisoner and needed a ride. So he throws the guy in the back of the truck and gets in beside him. They travel in the back with the 6 workers. He gets to a point where they get Peter to stop the truck and they both jump out. The policeman stops another car to hitch another ride to the police station in town. Only in Honduras!

I made chicken parmesan tonight and again I made the whole thing in the oven because it's easier than using the stove. I hate that it really heats up the kitchen but, I will do anything for a good meal. Normally I would fry the breaded chicken on the stove and then bake it with the sauce and cheese in the oven however, this worked out quite well.

Chicken Parmesan

You will need:

4 chicken breasts – butterflied and pounded flat

1 cup flour

2 eggs beaten

1 cup breadcrumbs

1 tbsp. Italian seasoning

¼ cup grated fresh parmesan

½ tsp. salt

½ tsp. pepper

½ tsp. chili flakes

2 tbsp. fresh parsley - chopped fine

½- ¾ cup grated mozzarella cheese

Olive oil

Sauce

14 oz. can of crushed tomatoes

1 tsp. chili flakes

1 tsp. dried oregano

Salt and pepper

2 cloves garlic crushed

2 tbsp. grated parmesan

1 tbsp. fresh chopped basil

1 tbsp. fresh chopped parsley

- Heat the oven to 375 degrees F.

- Step 1: Place your palm flat across the entire chicken breast and carefully slice until you almost come to the end. Open up the chicken like a book and place on a sheet of plastic wrap. Cover the top with another sheet of plastic and gently pound with a meat mallet or wine bottle. You are looking to make a large even piece of chicken.

- Step 2: Get your breading station ready. Place flour on a plate. In a bowl, beat eggs. On another plate mix breadcrumbs with Italian seasoning, grated parmesan, chili flakes and fresh chopped parsley.

- Step 3: Season chicken lightly with salt and pepper. Dip each side in the flour, then the egg, then the breadcrumb mixture. Press in the breadcrumbs to make a nice coating.

- Step 4: On a baking sheet, drizzle some olive oil and place cutlets on top. Drizzle some more olive oil on top of each cutlet. You would normally fry these in a pan with oil. In order to create a similar texture you must add some oil to the bottom and tops of cutlets.

- Step 5: Bake in hot oven for 10 minutes. Flip and bake 10 more minutes.

- Step 6: Take all ingredients for tomato sauce and mix in a bowl. You don't need to cook it. This also makes a great pizza sauce.

- Step 7: Remove chicken from oven. Top with some tomato sauce and sprinkle with mozzarella. Return to oven for another 10- 15 minutes to melt and brown cheese.

- Serve with pasta or a big salad or both.

☀ November 6, 2008

Peter went to Canada today and I am all alone for seven days in this giant house. I miss him already and he just left. Being here has really strengthened our relationship and we are pretty solid. I feel like we are closer than ever. I worry about him every day because stupid things happen all the time around here. Men behave like cowboys and they just constantly do macho things which often end in accidents or disasters. I hope everything is fine. I can't imagine being here without him, anywhere without him really. I am very lucky and I know it.

"If you're lucky and you know it clap your hands!"

☀ November 7, 2008

Peter called last night to tell me he arrived and everything is ok. I had a shitty night sleeping because he wasn't here. The dogs were also restless because he was not here. Peter told me the leaves are all turning color and the cold fall days make it necessary for him to wear a jacket for the first time in ages. He slept with blankets! I was so jealous!

The thought of being cold sounds so nice after being so hot. He said everything looks so different and unfamiliar and the stores look so big. I am missing my old normal life back in Canada. I don't miss my old job but I miss the modern comforts and having my own home. For some reason today seems hotter than ever. I know this is terrible but, I went to the web and found a countdown calendar and entered the date in 3 years when we can leave. I wanted to know how many days that was. I have 1009 days until I can leave. I am sick of being hot! I am sick of having a million mosquito bites! I want to go home! I wish I could manifest some way we could finish sooner than 1009 days. I am sad and so depressed.

☀ November 8, 2008

Today is another day and I am trying to snap out of my funk. I watched Manuel's children for a few minutes today. I saw Maria who is maybe 8 and Daniel who is maybe 6 or 7, walking around by the river with their dad's machete looking for crabs. They are often foraging for things their mother can use as bait for fishing. They are so young and yet so mature in so many ways. If you just consider this situation. In Canada no one would let their 7 and 8 year old kids hang around a river bank that has a 7 foot crocodile in it (if we had crocodiles in rivers in Canada). Not to mention you would probably get arrested if you let your kids walk around with a machete!

This is Daniel and Maria with the new baby

✳ November 9, 2008

It is the third day that Peter has been gone and I know he is having a good time. This thought makes me happy but I miss him and I don't like to be here all by myself.

Last night we had some rain and a lot of thunder and lightning. The rain scared Lulu and she was stuck to me like glue for the evening. Molli is perfectly happy and too deaf to be bothered. This morning it is sunny and pleasant. Everything has been watered so I don't have to do that however, the rain has made it very humid. It's the usual 30 degrees C and 72% humidity but it's just 7 am and that's pretty muggy for so early in the day. It is a Sunday morning and Sundays are always the best days because no one is here working and making noise or a mess or asking for something. I go and gather some more mangos... I should have counted how many I have used in total since I got here. I bet it has been in the hundreds. I want to freeze some more while they are still available. The locals say this was a great year because it was hotter than usual. (See I am not insane. Hotter than normal at the equator is saying something!) And the tree produced four rounds of fruit. Once the tree stops producing fruit it will rest until about December. Then it will flower and fruit again for another season. Even the trees are always pregnant down here!

✳ November 10, 2008

The two dogs that belong to Robelio and Gilberto (the watchmen) came bounding up to the door when I opened it this morning. Tigra who is always shy is even letting me touch her. Cheezpa (I call him Cheese Puff) was very happy today. Both his ears were standing straight up. He had the ticks removed and his ears were cleaned. He seems very relieved and full of playful energy. These really are just young dogs full of piss and vinegar. I am glad they are happy. Their coats are all looking good and they are no longer so terribly thin. I am glad in these small ways to help make them more comfortable and happy. Isn't it all just about a small gesture or tiny kindness here or there that makes a difference in the lives of others? It doesn't matter whether you are human or animal.

I feel so happy when I see them happy. It seems so strange that I feel so lost here most of the time. The only times I feel good are when I experience some joy from an animal or a beautiful flower or some natural discovery or the taste of something good. My senses are all connected. If it were not for those specks of spirit I would be in big trouble. I am really struggling to maintain my positive outlook and depression comes over me like a slap in the face for the weirdest things. I see something sad or hear a story that just puts me in a hole that I am finding harder and harder to climb out of.

I was looking at some pictures of my old house and noticed that it was such a cute little place. I never really appreciated how nice it was. I remember feeling that it was too small and always needed something repaired. Today I am feeling it was great and I miss it. I miss having my own little place where I can put things where I want to and make it pretty and my own. I have realized that my own place no matter how small is very critical to my happiness. It is so hard to live with other people no matter how big a house is. Even as a child I had my own place under the basement stairs where I created my own apartment, a place I could put the things that were important to me. A tiny little space filled with lovely things, decorated the way you want it, can be more beautiful than a palace that belongs to someone else. I always need a sense of home and I don't have that here right now. I am just sad. Sadness makes me quiet. It covers me. I don't want to talk about anything. Silence is a way you don't have to share. I am tired.

When I imagine being at the end of my life looking back over my time, the things I want to have accomplished are not things that are really grand or even important. They come down to a few simple things. I want to have been a good wife, a good partner to my husband... One half of a team of two! I want to have a beautiful home not in size but, in warmth and character. I want it to be said that I was a good mother. Now if you understand that I do not have any children this may seem a strange thing to want. Although I never had human children, I have always felt fulfilled from a maternal perspective because I have always had animals since I was a very young child. Each one of them sealed in my soul and critical to helping me to open my heart to the other humans I know. Lastly, I want to know I have had a handful of good friends. I don't need a million, just a few near and dear.

That's it really!

Be a good wife
Create a good home
Be a good mother
Be a good friend

I don't have a need to help the masses to do my part. I don't have it in me to work in grand ways. I just need a few intimate contacts; to touch a few important lives rather than to spread myself thin and be nothing to everyone I meet. I am a concentrated person, that's how I like it. Life is short. I hope to have a few good relationships and forget the rest.

✳ November 11, 2008

It's busy around here today. There are guys sanding the doors, plus guys working on some mechanical issues in the bodega. There are guys building the new house, plus the cleaning lady is here. A big dump truck just dropped off a big load of rocks and sand. It is crazy and noisy.

Everyone is bugging me. They know I am depressed and they are worried about me. I appreciate their concerns but, I don't want to talk about it. There is nothing to say. I have to figure out a way to snap out of it on my own. I can't continue to keep discussing why I can't get in a happy place. Why can't I ever just be quiet without people freaking out? Leave me be.

I ran out of propane today so the kitchen stove doesn't work. I made onion soup entirely in the oven. Since the oven was on, I made a loaf of French baguette to go with the soup. Thank God for the oven being electric and the barbeque (when it has propane). If I didn't have those I would be building a fire and cooking outside which I am not beyond doing. In my own house I want an electric stove. Anything you need to refill around here is dumb. It's been raining all day. This house is so dark on a rainy day even if all the lights are on.

I made some excellent chicken empanadas today. I also made some oatmeal chocolate chip cookies and I froze some of both for when Carly and Roger get back.

Chicken Empanadas

You will need:

Filling:
2 cups shredded chicken (4 breasts cooked and shredded into pieces)

1 dried ancho chili

½ onion – chopped fine

3 cloves garlic – minced/crushed

2 tsp. ground cumin

½ tsp. ground cinnamon

1 tomato – chopped finely

½ tsp. each salt and pepper

2 tbsp. fresh cilantro – chopped fine

2 tbsp. toasted pumpkin seeds

2 tbsp. hot sauce

¾ cup shredded old cheddar

½ lime – juiced

Optional: some chopped raisins soaked in a bit of rum

Dough:
2 cups flour

¾ cup masa – corn flour

2 tsp. sugar

½ tsp. salt

3 tbsp. shortening or lard

2 egg yolks

¾ cup warm water

- Step 1: In the food processor, add all the ingredients for the dough and process for 5 minutes until it creates a smooth dough. Wrap in plastic and leave in fridge at least 1 hour.

- Step 2: Make filling: In a dry fry pan, toast the chili on both sides. Then add to a blender with a ¼ cup hot water and blend well. In a bowl add shredded chicken, chili liquid, chopped onion, crushed garlic, cumin, cinnamon, chopped tomato, some salt and pepper, cilantro, pumpkin seeds, hot sauce, cheese and lime. Add rum soaked raisins if you like. Taste it and adjust for seasoning. You can also add a bit of olive oil to make it a bit stickier.

- Step 3: Role out the dough and cut into circles or you can divide dough into little balls and roll out each ball into a circle.

- Step 4: Fill with a small amount of filling. Wet the edges with water and seal. You can use a fork to make the edge decorative.

- Step 5: Fry in oil or bake and eat hot. They are so much better fried than baked. I wish they weren't.

You can also freeze these uncooked for another time.

The guys who sand the doors and windows have been here every day for weeks. They are so funny to watch. They are young guys maybe 17-18, maybe younger. I look at one guy and try to figure out his story. I guess that he has an older brother and a younger brother. I think that he must have an older brother because he is always mean to the dogs on the property. I think he must have an older brother that tortured him and so he tortures anything younger than him or anything defenceless like a dog. I also think he has a younger brother because his shoes are too small. I just get the impression he would steal his younger brother's shoes when he leaves in the morning. I think how life is really just always about LOVE. The kind you get and the kind you don't. It shapes everything about us.

I went to see the puppies and their eyes are open today. They are getting nice and chubby. Manuel's wife showed me that they are eating now. So I will go buy some puppy food and another container to drop off food along with the adult dog food. More mouths to feed!

Manuel's wife came near me and I noticed she has a huge open sore on the top of her foot. She explained she also has another one on her hip. The woman has five children and works so hard to provide a home for her family. She has no front teeth and just looks so tired. I know she sees a doctor once in a while because they all get dressed up and go next door to the Finca (which is a children's ranch or orphanage) that has a doctor on staff. That sore is pretty badly infected. I don't know if it was from a bite or what it came from. I look at her and wonder how old she is? She looks like she could be in her fifties but, I assume she is in her thirties since she just had a baby recently. Maybe, she is in her forties? I wouldn't want to be a fertile female of any species in Honduras. Something is always trying to hump you and get you pregnant.

I watched little Manuelito, who is maybe two years old, walking past the kitchen window with his mother. He was carrying a small pail which he filled entirely full of mangos. I watch him carrying the pail that looks like it could almost be half his weight and his mother walking right behind him. You have to literally pull your own weight around here.

Later on I saw Daniel walking past the kitchen with a huge bundle of sticks on his back for the fire. He works very hard on his chores and usually looks very serious doing what is necessary to help his family in many ways and becoming a man. I think he is quite sweet. Maybe Peter can build him a cart for the wood as a Christmas gift?

✳ November 12, 2008

It poured rain today… a torrential downpour. Before the rain started I took the dogs out for a pee and Lulu didn't want to go because of the loud thunder. I was glad when she eventually did. Because once the rain came, I would have had a hard time to get her to go out even if I had an umbrella over her. It was also really windy which I love. Finally a nice breeze but, the water just pours into the house through the bottom of all of the bedroom doors that lead out to the pool area. I have soaked at least 12 towels wiping up the water. We need a squeegee like they have at swimming pools. When the rain comes you use the squeegee to push it out and then you only have to wipe up a bit of water. The water is really dangerous because when the tiles are wet they are very slippery.

The wind and rain were so violent it almost felt like it could be a hurricane. Wow! After about an hour it stopped. I went to look at my kitchen garden and the flower beds are filled right up to the rim with water. It looks like a swimming pool for basil plants.

An hour later it rained really hard just like it did before and then just as quickly stopped. The sea is very choppy when there is a storm coming and after a big rainfall it is fun to go to see what has washed up on the beach. Sometimes you can find some neat sea glass. I walked down the beach in front of the house with the waves loud and crashing in my ears and the wind blowing pretty hard. It is truly disheartening to see how much garbage ends up on the beach after a storm. It is like seeing the worst part of our disposable North American society reaching these remote Honduran beaches. The number of those giant plastic pop bottles, flip flops and every kind and size of plastic container is ridiculous. So much plastic pollutes the sea.

I am always fascinated by how many people in North America as well as in Honduras have decided that they cannot afford the high cost of fruits and vegetables in their diets but, they find it possible to buy giant bottles of pop. Isn't there something so wrong about this? The devastating consequences of this kind of diet will be felt for years and maybe generations. The obvious sign to me is just the sheer number of people of all ages, who have lost their front teeth and walk everywhere with a giant bottle of pop in their hands at all times of day. When did I get to be so bitter?

The third power failure happened today around 7 pm and the watchmen think it won't come back on until morning. How do they know this? I wonder. Manuel told me to get my candles ready for the evening. Great, I am all alone in the big house and there is no sound in the house, no TV, and no computer but, since there has been so much rain the sound of a million frogs are lulling me to sleep. I guess they are happy it's wet outside.

The night was long. The wind eventually died down and it got very hot even with all the windows open. The frogs were so loud they woke me up at midnight. I also had to move Molli to the bed on the floor because she normally sleeps against my legs and I was sweating to death from the heat coming off of her.

What is in store for today? My boy (Peter) is coming home tonight. I am very glad and very excited to see him.

It rained a bit this morning. It is 26 degrees in my room which is fantastic and pleasant. It's raining lightly again as I write this.

It is some kind of holiday here today although I have no idea for what. They have lots of them. Once I learned it was a holiday I didn't expect anyone to be here, but the cleaning lady came, the guy who drives the backhoe came, and all the sanding guys came. So don't ask me. I don't understand much of what goes on in this country.

I went over to see the puppies today. After the big rain I wanted to check on how they were doing. I found them under the boat, sort of dry, lying on the original dog bed I gave them. The bed was completely filthy. I wipe off all the sand on the puppies. I cleaned the second dog bed and put them all there for safe keeping. I then brushed off the filthy bed, hosed off the dirt and sand, and took it back to the house to give it a good wash. I came back a few hours later with it all freshly laundered and dried. Honestly, I don't know what they did to get it that dirty. I thought the kid was sleeping on it but, maybe not. Those dogs could certainly all use a bath. Imagine what they would say if I asked them if I could wash their dogs? Maybe another day I will.

I am appalled (yes appalled!) at the fact that everybody, including the cleaning lady just throw their garbage on the property wherever they are. If you gave someone a pop, they would drink it and then throw the bottle on the ground. We keep the empty bottles and return them when we go back to buy more and yet they still just toss them on the ground. We have to put large garbage containers everywhere and constantly tell them to put their garbage in the bins. It doesn't even dawn on them that they should not just throw it on the ground wherever they are. It is terrible when you drive into town. You see litter everywhere. They do have garbage pick-up but most people just throw their garbage wherever they are, or they burn it on their front lawns. It is heartbreaking to see them throw plastic pop bottles in the river and then watch them get washed up on the beaches when there is a storm. I understand that these are small issues for a country with big concerns and garbage is hardly the most important priority but, it just breaks your heart to see it everywhere. When you see them burning Styrofoam and plastic on their front lawns with their babies in diapers all running around again you realize how much needs to be done to help these people understand they need to protect themselves, their land, their water and their precious coral reefs. One step at a time! One good act at a time and they will hopefully learn to appreciate their land, their resources, their wildlife and water. I really hope so.

❄ November 14, 2008

Peter is back and I had a great sleep last night. I think I really like the rainy season. It's windy and cooler and I feel much better now that I am not sweating constantly. I am still itchy though. If someone could fix that I would be eternally grateful.

I saw a beautiful brown horse on the property this morning and I wondered where it came from. I thought it was a present for me. I later found out it belonged to Joe and he just brought it to graze. Too bad for me.

I think the mangos are pretty much finished. It has been mind boggling to think of how many people have enjoyed the benefits of that one tree. Every visitor to the house and every worker has taken 6-8 in their T-shirt slings every day. Not to mention all the cows that spent their days just trying to make a run for the area near the tree. They would sneak in and quickly steal as many as they could eat before being chased off by the watchmen. It always reminded me of the pictures of Farmer McGregor chasing Peter Rabbit from his patch of prized vegetables. I was always rooting for the cows, by the way.

Oh, it is such a beautiful day here. I find it hilarious that all the Hondurans are all walking around freezing and wearing jackets.

I got the propane tank for the stove back today. It has been about 4 days since I have been able to use the stove top. I am amazed at how inventive and creative I can be with the microwave, the oven and the grill. I normally never use the microwave for anything except maybe melting butter or defrosting hamburger buns. I learned I can make a perfectly round egg for an Egg McMuffin like sandwich. I put a little oil in a round dish, crack an egg, and microwaved it for 1 minute. I grill a piece of salami or bacon and place on a toasted bun. Just like McDonalds.

I also learned how to make onion soup entirely in the oven. I roasted all the onion slices and then added the broth. Once the soup had cooked and was bubbly, I spooned it into individual ramekins, added the toast and cheese, and melt that in the oven. I made a chicken soup one night entirely on the barbeque (grill). I can be quite resourceful when I have to be. If you have to eat you should eat the best you can!

We had 2 power failures today. It happens all the time so I am getting used to it. Today I don't even care because it has cooled off so beautifully. I feel like a completely different person in this weather. I feel great.

❄ November 15, 2008

This morning the sky was all dark and foreboding. There was a little light rain last night which is unusual since it's normally so heavy. It is 6 am and there is still no power and now I am worried about my nice little collection of goodies in the freezer. I hope they are not spoiled. Manuel saw that I was up and turned on the generator for a while so I could make some breakfast. It appeared that everything was fine in the freezer. The rain has started up again.

I did 2 workouts today. I did a good job because I was just pouring water from my forehead, my arms and my legs. The power is still not back on. It is 9 am and we are still using the generator power. Maybe I will make a quiche today with some leftovers from my roast chicken and my leftover roasted vegetables.

It's 11:10 am and there is still no power. They have turned off the generator and now it's getting hot and sticky. I went out to take the dogs for a pee and I noticed a nice big fat tarantula crawling up the wall of the pool shack. This one is quite a bit larger than the last one I saw. Hmm, I have seen tarantulas, a giant horned beetle, a scorpion, bats, poisonous snakes in the grass, mosquitoes... This place is just full of fun things. People wonder why I don't like to leave all the doors open at night. Yeah, I am weird. I just don't want scary shit coming into bed with me. This is the kind of place where you get ideas for kids' scary stories. Scary stories with monsters that come into your room at night and live under your bed!

Enrique the backhoe driver was over at the bodega and when I told him about the spider he was only too happy to come over and kill it. I could not kill something that big and squishy. I wish they would just remove it to somewhere safe and happy for all spiders where they could live in peace but, that is the not the way things are done here. If he could have shot it to see it explode he would have. I have a bad feeling that someday spiders are going to come after me, like in the Harry Potter stories, for killing that mama!

The wind has just picked up. I feel like I could be on Cape Cod on a cloudy summer day. It feels so damn good to be cool and it just amazes me how quickly the weather can change around here.

2 pm and the power finally came back on. Wow, that was a long one!

I feel really good today. I feel dry and comfortable in my own clothes. I am happy hanging out with my two little pooches. They are so cute when they sleep on their little pads in the kitchen when I am busy cooking.

I made an excellent quiche with all my leftover chicken and roasted vegetables. I had some Swiss chard I had grown, roasted potatoes, tomatoes, onions, garlic, chicken, parmesan cheese, fresh herbs and spices. It was very good and I have some left for tomorrow's lunch.

9 pm and there is another power failure. Come on! This is becoming a drag but, then it comes back on in 45 minutes. They must have heard me.

✳ November 16, 2008

Karl and Judy invited Al and Carrie over to their place for breakfast this morning. When I saw Carrie afterwards I asked her how her breakfast was and she said it was lovely. They had nice coffees and she had toast with homemade flower jam. I wonder what kind of flower? Maybe it was hibiscus jam? I know they make tea from it. Why not jam? Inviting people for breakfast is such a neat thing to do for a change. I might have to consider having a breakfast party sometime. Holy cow, I am feeling good. I never want to have parties or invite anyone over.

We were at Rogues Galleria on the beach road. Four guys came in with cowboy hats playing giant guitars and an accordion. They were singing and playing Mexican Ranchero Music. We had never seen them before and we paid them 100 lempira ($5) to play 3 songs for us. It was loads of fun to have live entertainment. All the locals were killing themselves laughing at how funny it all was. They think that kind of music is hilarious.

Just before you drive into Trujillo you cross the Santa Fe River. This is a large river and it gets lots of use. The women who do not have running water in their homes come to stand in their bras and panties and bathe in it. You drive by and they are soaping up their hair, in their underwear washing all their bits and pieces, la-de-da, like they are not standing out in the open. You turn your head and there is another woman on the rocks washing clothes. You see people drive their trucks right in it for a car wash. You even see the fire truck drive in it to fill up with water. How easy is it for me to take for granted a house to live in with running water and privacy to wash my dirty laundry or my dirty self.

Manuel's wife showed me her foot and the huge gaping sore is even bigger and not healing. She also has some kind of red rash all over her body. She said she went to see the doctor next door at the Finca and he gave her some cream which made her foot worse and she never had that rash before. I freaked out when I saw it. I begged Joe and Peter to help her do something. Peter will take her to the hospital tomorrow morning. They will leave at 5 am because otherwise there will be a huge line up of people. The healthcare is free to residents but most have a hard time getting to the doctor or hospital and then they have no money for the medicine when it is prescribed. She thinks she needs 500 lempira which is about $20. Peter said he will give them the money and drive her and Manuel to the hospital. She has such a bad infection I am worried that if it gets worse she might lose the foot or the leg. It was that gross.

❊ November 17, 2008

Peter took Manuel and his wife to the hospital early this morning. When they got back Peter told me that she got a needle and some pills and she is already feeling better. I feel better.

Carly and Roger got back this afternoon and I made Greek potatoes, lemon chicken, with a tomato, pepper and onion salad, and an artichoke dip as an appetizer. We also had banana cake for dessert and I sort of made some banana rum ice cream to go with it. It was a good cheat. I bought some store bought vanilla ice cream added some squished bananas and some rum. It was surprisingly good. I must say it was quite the fiesta.

It is cloudy today which is too bad because it was beautiful for the last three days and now it's cloudy just when they get here.

❋ November 18, 2008

This morning something wonderful happened. While I was washing dishes a beautiful hummingbird flew right up to the window directly in front of where I was standing. She just hovered there and we stared at each other for a few seconds and then she flew away. Sometimes something so simple can just makes you stop what you are doing and stare in amazement. Seeing a hummingbird is like seeing a fairy. It is magical when they are so close in front of you. If you don't pay attention it's gone in the blink of an eye. There are plenty of things that I can almost not bear about being here and just when I am not paying attention something wonderful happens to make me believe again. Even in this hard, rough place every once in a while something makes me hold my breath, stop what I am doing and smile.

I saw Daniel, Manuel's son, combing the puppies' coats and kissing and hugging them. I found a little comb I had for lice that was very fine and gave it to him. I told him I was watching him taking good care of his dogs and that he was a good boy for doing a very nice thing. He is such a sweet little man/boy, all serious most of the time, and it was nice to see him being loving and playful.

We went to a birthday party in town today. I am not someone who likes a birthday party at any time. Too many people, too loud, too crowded. I get all claustrophobic and just want to get out. We went to a birthday party at a bar in the Cristales neighborhood for a friend of Roger's. It was really hot when we got inside and there were so many people all jammed in. At one point the music was so loud I thought my heart was going to explode. It was like standing in front of the speakers at a concert. I tried to move over to a corner of the room but, the room kept filling up with more people. People were dancing and having a great time but the room just got hotter and tighter. We left after about an hour and I was truly thankful when everyone was ready to go. I shot out of that place like a bat out of hell. I just don't see how that is fun. Even when I was younger I never went to clubs or bars often because it was just too loud and claustrophobic.

❋ November 19, 2008

This morning a hummingbird flew right into the house! It flew around for about an hour. All the doors were open and I even hung a hummingbird feeder in front of the open double doors to lure him down to get out. He would not fly low enough to find his way out. I turned off all the ceiling fans so he wouldn't get hurt.

At one point I thought for sure he was going to fly out. He flew down to the wide open double doors. He flew right to the stained glass window with calla lilies on it as if to take a drink and was literally 3 inches away from freedom and then flew up again. He was flying around and then, he simply ran out of gas and just floated right to the floor. I took a light tea towel and let it fall on him and I gently picked him up. I carried his tiny body out to the back deck and opened the towel and he stared at me for a second and then just flew off. I was really scared to put the towel on him because I thought I would hurt him. He was so small and delicate but I did it! I felt exhilarated. I can't believe I had a hummingbird in my hands and I looked at him up close. When does that ever get to happen?

And then 10 minutes later Lulu rolled herself in diesel fuel which made her unbelievably stinky and dirty. I had to wash her a few times in some skunk shampoo we had. We went from one extreme to the next in 10 minutes.

I checked on Manuel's wife today and she looks so much better. Her rash is gone and her leg is starting to look a bit better.

It is raining again.

I made some chili oil and some basil oil. I think I will make some sweet potato ravioli today with some balsamic vinegar and use my oils on top.

Basil Oil

1 ½ cups packed fresh basil leaves
1 cup olive oil

- Blend for 1 minute in a blender. Add to a small saucepan and heat on low until it just starts to bubble around the sides. Let stand to room temperature. Strain and store in fridge.

Chili Oil

2 cups olive oil
4 tsp. dried chili flakes

- Heat oil and chili flakes in saucepan on low temperature for 5 minutes. Cool to room temperature and store in sealed container on counter or fridge.

Last night we watched the movie Lonesome Dove. I was totally bummed after watching it. I found it too sad and heartbreaking. It is the story of the struggles in building the American west. It reminds me of being here. This place is just like the wild west. Everything is hard. Nothing happens easily, nothing.

Solita was lying in the champa this morning. (It's a little covered hut). The champa was the only place she could lie down that was dry. Wobey, the brat dog, was lying on our hammock, rolling around and getting it all nice and dirty. Manuel has started to give away the puppies or maybe they sell them. I don't know. One of the backhoe drivers is taking a little black one. While he was working he decided to keep the puppy in a big tire that was on the ground. It was a good idea to keep the puppy contained however, it howled and cried. I heard the howling from inside the house. I am like a mother hearing a child crying in distress. I had to go find out where the crying was coming from. When I found the wee pup I had to pick him up and soothe him. He was immediately quiet and fell right to sleep. I found a blanket and put him on the blanket. I explained to the guy that he needs to be nice to his dog and that he must buy him dog food. He cannot just leave him alone to fend for himself. He promised he would and I ran into the house and got him a bag full of some dog food to take with him. I again begged him to feed him real dog food. He smiled and agreed. Whether he will is another story. I felt so bad that this innocent little dog would very quickly be facing a life with all the hardships and traumas that dogs face here. I have to let it go. I can't feed them all and I can't fix this issue so you just hope they are treated kindly and get fed. Just let it go!

This morning Carly wanted to go over to see Manuel's house to see if she could help with something that would improve their conditions. Their house has 2 rooms and a washroom. There is one room to sleep in and the other room is like their main living room with a sink in it. They have a wood stove outside on the front porch and a little table out on the porch as well. These houses were originally built for a single watchman to live in but, there is now a family here. They have electricity, running water, a good roof and a new TV. Carly wants to see if we can get some countertops put in for them so they can have a place to prepare meals.

Sometimes when you are just walking down the hallway of the house you look down and you think there might be a bug walking down the hall and when you look closer you realize it is a teeny tiny crab! There are crabs just walking down your hallway!

Carly and I went to a new grocery store today in nearby Tacoa and it was pretty good. We found lots of things we can't get in Trujillo but it is a recently opened store and they still have lots of bare shelves. I am sure in time it will get better.

I found something funny in the lawn today. When I was in Canada I grew a small plant called a sensitive plant. Everyone that saw that little plant was fascinated by it. It was a lacy little plant and when you touch the leaves they fold up. I have also heard some people call it a prayer plant. In Honduras there are thousands of them and they grow in the lawn between the grasses. In one place something is a weed and in another place it is an exotic plant.

We found a giant crab in the pool today. We told Manuel and he was very pleased to remove it. Then he took it home and ate it.

I am going to make chicken lasagna today with homemade noodles. When in Honduras you use the things you can get in Honduras. My weird lasagna had sweet potato and parmesan on one layer. Chicken and spices on another layer and some melted cheese. It sounds kind of gross when I think about it but, it was pretty good.

✳ November 21, 2008

It's a nice day today. It's not raining, it's cool and comfortable. Nothing stupid or exciting or unbelievable has happened. Yesterday when I was at Rogues Galleria Lucita gave me a bag of lemons. They were wild lemons and they are the size of grapefruits and the skin is very bumpy. When you cut them open there are hundreds of seeds. It is surprising how many seeds are in each lemon. The ratio of seeds to pulp is maybe 50/50. They do taste like a lemon but they are not as tart as the smaller Eureka lemons we get in North America. I will make some lemon bars and I will share them with Lucita. I want her to try them because she thinks lemons don't taste nice and she cannot imagine them used for something sweet like a dessert.

I made the lemon bars and although they are not as tart as I like them they were still good. Lucita was pleasantly surprised that they were good and she admitted that she liked them.

I made a fantastic pork loin in apples, olive oil and spices. I served it with some roasted vegetables that I sprinkled with cumin salt. You can add other things to salt like chilies or herbs as well. If you add something wet then you need to make sure you dry out the salt before storing it.

Cumin Salt Seasoning

2 tsp. cumin seeds – toasted
1 dried bay leaf
4 tsp. brown sugar
½ tsp. hot smoked paprika
3 tsp. sea salt
1 tsp. pepper

- Grind the seeds and bay leaf in a mortar and pestle or a coffee mill. Mix in the other ingredients and it can be sprinkled on fish or chicken or even vegetables.

It rained from 3 pm this afternoon until about 8:30 pm. It came down so hard that the workers were actually stranded here. Peter was also stranded in Trujillo. When you have a heavy rainfall, the rivers get too high and you cannot cross over the planchas (which are a type of cement bridge that you can drive your car over). Normally the water just gently washes over the planchas and it is not a problem for a car to drive through. When there is a bad storm, the water level over the planchas gets too high and the current is too rough for a car to drive through. So you are stuck until the rain stops and the river calms down. Roger's was the last vehicle that made it back from Santa Fe. When he crossed, the water level was up to the headlights on his truck!

This is what happens when you try to cross the planchas when the water level is too high

This is what happens to the planchas – normally a car can drive over the river on the cement plancha however, when there is a storm the rains make the river so high that you cannot cross.

Here is what happens when you try and you should have waited. This car got swept right into the river.

Carrie was at our house visiting and couldn't get back to her place. Carrie lives just a few miles down the road but, there are two planchas to cross so she stayed the night. When building a home in Honduras, always build a home with extra guest rooms because not only will people want to come to visit you on vacations but, you never know who just might get stuck and have to stay the night. The workers were all stuck here and we had to figure out something to feed them since they couldn't get home for dinner. We made some beans and rice which is some-thing they all eat. It's strange because the Hondurans do not like to eat their food spicy. Apparently, they said they make their beans and rice with margarine and sugar which truly sounds disgusting to me. I literally had to hold myself back while cooking from adding other things to this meal because it just looked so plain. I am sure they didn't like the plain white rice we made (we don't use margarine so we didn't have any in the house) but, it was hot and they were cold and they ate it. They were all wearing jackets and freezing and I was feeling so comfortable in the cooler weather. Later that evening all the workers were able to get back to their homes.

I can't imagine what the heat of this place would be like if you were going through menopause.

Roger was driving in his truck earlier in the day before the rain started and saw someone cutting down a palm tree. He bought the heart of palm from them and I made a nice salad with it for part of our dinner. It was such a nice present when he brought it out of his truck. Peter finally managed to get home at 9:45 pm. I was very relieved when he got back. I guess he could have stayed over at the Christopher Columbus hotel if he had to but, I prefer it when he is home with me.

✳ November 22, 2008

I looked at Peter the other day and realized he is officially like a local because he always carries his blackberry in a Ziploc bag to protect it from the rain like all the Hondurans do.

Mould just grows on your shit here. I left the dog collar on the bookshelf a while back and today I looked at it and it had black mould growing on it. Some of my shoes in the closet have mould growing on them. It's quite weird to have something in your house getting mouldy. We have decided to hook up our dehumidifier in the closet to see if this will help.

I wish I could buy whole wheat flour here or any other kind of flour but the only thing I can buy is soft white flour or corn flour (Masa). Today I will make fresh pasta, with a tomato sauce, garlic bread, salad and an artichoke dip as an appetizer.

Everyone else has gone to La Ceiba this morning and I have stayed home. It is such a long day when you go and the more stops you have to make the longer the day gets. I just could not leave the dogs for 12 hours or even longer. It is raining and if the rain delays them in any way they will have problems getting back. I am thankful I am here and not on the road.

I never thought I would miss Canada but I really do this morning. It is fall there and the maple leaves are probably turning red and yellow. The cold sunny days in Ontario can be really nice. I never realized how many things that grow so well in Canada are impossible to grow here and on the other side there are lots of great things that you can grow here that you cannot grow there unless you have a greenhouse. The first snowfall of the season is always the prettiest but, I don't miss driving in the crappy winter storms with all that slush and sleet. Travelling anywhere when it is minus 25 degrees C is certainly not my idea of fun. I do have to say I am enjoying the rainy season so much more than the stagnant heat and oppression of the summer. I think now that it is cooler I could probably try to start some seeds that I couldn't get to germinate before. In my head I think of starting seeds in the springtime but the fall here might be more like the spring as I know it from a temperature perspective. I might have to think of gardening upside down.

Instead of having squirrels running all over your back lawn you have black and white iguanas or little green lizards. Sometimes it still surprises me when I see them.

I found a giant frog in my closet this afternoon. I got a big bucket and captured him and then let him go in the garden. How do these things get in here? I walked down to the other side of the house and found a little green tree frog climbing up Carly and Roger's bedroom door. I guess it's frog season in the house.

✳ November 23, 2008

It rained all night long and all day today. When the rain stopped the grass looked like it was a big pond. There were cranes walking across the lawn which only added to the image. The river flooded over to the area where the new house is going to be built. There were fish jumping on the lawn because the river rose so high it spilled over onto the grass. Manuel's wife is trying to catch tilapia flopping across the grass. It is actually quite a funny sight.

This is the river when it is overflowing

At the back of the house, the tile path to the beach is filled right up to the top edge of the stone in water. Actually the water is spilling over the edge like a garden fountain. All the flower beds are filled right up to their tops with water and the plants are under at least 6 inches of water. If there is anything that can act as a bucket, it is full today.

Tonight the rain continued on. It was the heaviest rain we have had yet. We used every towel in the house to soak up the water that poured in under the doors. I took a big fall near one of the doors because I slipped on the wet tiles. I hit so hard I thought I broke my arm. Luckily I did not. The thought of having to go to a Honduran hospital didn't excite me. Carly and Roger have to catch a plane tomorrow. They didn't want to get stuck so they headed out for San Pedro Sula this afternoon and within 10 minutes of them leaving the big heavy rain came. They could not have timed it better. If they left even a few minutes later they would have been stuck. Rumour was that they had 10 guys holding hands on one of the planchas to form a wall so Roger could drive over the plancha. I don't know if that is true or not but, it was pretty crazy rain.

✳ November 24, 2008

This morning the rain has finally stopped but there is water pooled everywhere. There are trees down and some have washed into the Mahoguay River that flows into the ocean. There is damage to the road coming to the property. We cannot drive out to the road because of the damage near the front gate. We might be able to get a quad out but not a larger vehicle. The river has taken out a huge amount of the river bank and now the river is much wider. You realize the incredible force and destructive power of water.

This is the damage done to the road coming into the property

Trees have been washed down the river.

The sides of the river have been eroded by the storm.

After the excitement of this morning I decided to make donuts. Peter said he missed the donuts from Tim Horton's in Canada and wished he could sit down and have a coffee and a donut. They were actually quite amazing. How can warm fried dough coated in chocolate and coconut glaze taste anything other than fantastic?

Yeast Donuts

¾ cup milk scalded
¼ cup butter
1/3 cup sugar
2 tsp. dry yeast
1/3 cup warm water
4 cups sifted flour
1 tsp. grated fresh nutmeg
2 eggs
oil for frying

- In a medium bowl, stir together the hot milk, butter and sugar, stir to dissolve the sugar and let cool to warm.
- In a small bowl, add warm water and yeast. Wait 5 minutes until yeast activates and gets foamy, add to the cooled milk mixture.
- Add eggs to the milk mixture and beat until combined. Add flour and nutmeg and mix until you cannot continue to mix in the bowl. Turn out mixture onto the counter and knead dough to incorporate all the flour. Knead the dough 4 minutes until smooth.
- Place in a buttered bowl and cover with plastic wrap. Let rise until doubled (approximately 45 minutes -1 hour).
- On a lightly floured surface, roll out to ½ inch in thickness. Cut into circles. Set aside on floured surface for 30-40 minutes to slightly rise again.
- Heat 1 inch of oil in a heavy bottomed pot to 350 degrees F and fry a few at a time. Fry until brown and flip over to cook other side. Remove from oil and place on paper towel to absorb excess oil.
- Dip into chocolate glaze or coconut glaze and top with shredded coconut. You can even dip in cinnamon sugar. Serve with coffee and eat warm.

Coconut Glaze:
2 cups icing sugar, 6 tbsp. milk and a drop of coconut extract.

Chocolate Glaze:
2 cups icing sugar, 4 tbsp. cocoa powder, 6 tbsp. milk, 1 tbsp. vanilla or rum.

It's raining again. It rained all night long and now all morning long however, it's not the torrential violent rain that it was yesterday, just a softer kinder rain. This rain doesn't pour into the house. This is good because I have just finished washing and drying all the towels I used yesterday.

You know there is something to be said for paying taxes and having a bit of irritating snow in your life. If there was just something in between nicer weather most of the time and not paying so much in taxes!

The rain has stopped finally and it's almost chilly. Holy shit I said it, I am almost cold. It is 23 degrees C and when there is a breeze it almost feels like I could put on a sweatshirt. I love the fashions here when it gets this cold. Some people will be wearing winter jackets and other people who don't have winter coats will wear towels wrapped around their shoulders like a shawl. I am sure they could not even imagine minus 25 degrees C in their wildest nightmares.

Let's see what today has in store for us!

We were able to get a ride into town today. We had to walk past the front gate and over the broken bridge in order to get to a car. One of the workers is driving us into town. It has been 3 days since the big rain and we are out of many food basics. When we got into town there was no milk, no sliced bread, no sugar and only a few vegetables. I could get some onions, garlic, some terrible looking carrots, a couple of potatoes and a few apples. There were no tomatoes, no peppers, no lettuce and we had to go to three stores to finally find some eggs. This is three days after a moderate storm. Imagine what it would be like after a really bad storm or a hurricane.

My arm is still sore from my fall but it is otherwise not damaged. I am sure I will live.

I made a great dinner tonight... a chicken soup or stew really. It had chicken, onions, garlic, white wine, rice and potatoes. (Sounds like all the things I could get in town, doesn't it? Well... that's how you have to cook here.) I could not buy bread so I made some really great buns. They were so tender because I added some cooked potato to the dough, which is an old fashioned baking secret. After dinner I happened to look up on the wall over the sink in the kitchen and there were a thousand mosquitoes and other little bugs. Nature is so weird. Out of the blue something odd just occurs. I am sure there are logical reasons for all of these anomalies that I am simply unaware of. Obviously there were conditions that just made the situation ideal for this to happen. In Canada, there were often strange infestations of grasshoppers, or lady bugs or mayflies. One day you just look outside and there are a million mayflies. Why?

The water has dried up from all the lawns and the sun finally came out today. Yeah!

We finally found the dehumidifier in the container. We plugged it in and a poof of dust and hair along with some dead flies blew out the top! The cloud landed all over poor Peter. When he opened up the machine, it appeared that a mouse must have got into it while it was in the container (or in our house just before the move) and died. The extreme heat of being in the container for a few months must have disintegrated the mouse into dust and hair. It was pretty funny!

When you pack a container for an overseas trip, they tell you to make sure everything is packed extremely well (more securely than you normally would for a move across town) to survive the long bumpy journey across the water. They also tell you not to pack any food whatsoever because there are lots of mice that are only too happy to hitch a ride and eat all your stuff. Once they get in they can do some nice damage along the way. I did bring some food things but everything was in glass and metal containers. There was nothing packed in plastic or cardboard and none of the food I had brought showed signs of rodents trying to get at it. I am wondering if perhaps it was a mouse from the old house. Not impossible to imagine since we lived on a huge lot that backed onto a forest and they did try to get in during the cold winters. Once the mouse was removed, the machine was working fine and we hope it will help with the mould on our clothes and shoes in the closet.

I had a few lemons left. Today when I cut into one, there were so many seeds there was hardly any fruit and the seeds were sprouting right in the lemon. I had never seen that before.

Today we took the dogs out for a pee but we didn't want to open our bedroom doors which could let mosquitoes in. So we used the doors of the bedroom next to ours and we noticed a funny thing. There were mushrooms growing in the wood of the stained glass window. Mushrooms were growing on the inside of the house! You think there might be some moisture issues down here?

Hmm?? What shall I make for dinner tonight....chicken or chicken? I should just have brought down chicken cookbooks.

※ November 27, 2008

I glanced out of the kitchen window this morning and saw a beautiful brown and white mustang. He was standing just past the river on the property. I took a few carrots to see if I could feed him. I approached slowly with kind words and an outstretched hand and he just trotted off. I went back to the house and got on a quad and drove right past him and there was no problem. I sat on the quad and tried to give him the carrots and once again he was not interested in me. Maybe no one has ever given him a carrot? Maybe he doesn't know what a carrot is? I am starting to feel I just have no luck with the equine variety of animal in Honduras. I watched him for a few minutes and then just left him alone. You never know what you will see walking around the front yard.

I decided to make an apple strudel today. In the end, the dough was terrible and the apples had no flavour. Note to self: Don't make that recipe again.

Today there was no water at the house. I found out later that the reason we had no water is there was a crack in the water pipe at the front gate. Someone is coming out to fix it. There is also a leak in the pool so the water level is down and the water in the pool is green because of all the rain we have had. I guess the algae went into hyper-drive?

The bridge at the front of the property is still out, so we can't drive any vehicles out or in. There is a large bridge out near Tacoa, so there is very little food being delivered into Tacoa or Trujillo. Could anything else happen? Fire or perhaps locusts?

I came out to the living room this morning and I saw Lulu looking out the glass doors to the pool and there was the cutest little green lizard on the other side of the door. It was such an adorable picture.

Lulu and the little green lizard

The good news is that it's not raining today. After all, it is the rainy season. The sun is so nice for a change. It was a beautiful morning. I found a little yellow and green sparrow in the bedroom next to ours today. I just opened the bedroom doors to the outside patio and out she flew! That was easy! I have decided that birds flying in your house are a sign of good luck and an omen for something wonderful about to happen! And I must say again it is a beautiful day - crystal clear blue skies, civilized warm temperatures and very low humidity. So I will take that.

I made peanut butter cookies and lime squares. I gave some to Judy and Karl next door and some to Manuel for his family. They were pretty darn delicious.

Manuel walked right up to me in the car port. He slipped off his rubber boot and swung his leg over the railing to show me. His feet and legs were all white and had sores on them. They looked like your hands get when you are in the bath too long. Manuel told me in a confident voice it was because of too much water. I was wondering how I could help. I looked at him and nodded my head and then went inside. I went on line to see if I could make some kind of powder to dry and soothe his sore feet. Sure enough I found a recipe for a healing foot powder and I promptly made up a batch for him. Baking soda, corn starch and tee tree oil. I also found some healing natural oil in my cupboard with things like mint, lavender, rosemary and tee tree oil in it. I brought it from Canada and it is for things like bug bites and itches. So I added some of that oil to my powder as well. I then had to create a shaker of some kind for him. I took a jam jar and poked holes in the lid and turned it into a large powder shaker. I brought it over to him and showed him how to use it and he was very pleased but I also got the impression that this was exactly what he expected me to do. I think they think I am some kind of medicine woman because they are starting to tell me when anything is wrong with the dogs or when they have any weird things wrong with them.

✳ November 28, 2008

Today was another absolutely gorgeous day. It was sunny and 27 degrees C, with no humidity at all. There was a nice breeze and not too many mosquitoes. I sat under an umbrella at the pool and finished Anne of Green Gables. Great book and a perfect day!

✳ November 29, 2008

Another sunny day! It hasn't rained in 3 days and today is the fourth. The people that are building the new house are coming today to see if they can start again. Now that the rain has stopped and the ground has dried out they can carry on.

My first moonflowers opened tonight! Very exciting and on a night with a full moon too!

✳ November 30, 2008

Our run of sunny days seems to be over. I woke up this morning to the sound of light rain on the roof. Oh well at least it's not snowing like it is in Toronto.

I pulled up all the basil today and replanted some more. I will make a batch of pesto that I will freeze into an ice cube tray. I love having stuff in the freezer for a rainy day.

It actually turned out to be a glorious day. After the rain this morning it cleared right up. I brought some rye flour with me from Canada so I made rye bread. I had leftover Red River breakfast cereal which I also added to another bread recipe. I took the cooked cereal and added it to some yeast, water, honey, salt and flour. It created a nice loaf of grain bread.

It is not that difficult to create your own recipes. It's just cooking and baking. If you screw it up just throw it out and try again.

Lulu is so funny when she runs around the pool with her little fuzzy toy. We call her Missy Pissy Pants.

We saw the crocodile in the river again today. We went over the bridge and looked down in the water and there he was just silently swimming past the bridge. Holy shit! I can't get over that a crocodile could just walk up on your lawn. Now he never has, thank God. But really I wouldn't leave my dogs to go walking near the water's edge. Like anything else you take it in stride when it's a part of your neighborhood but, this is just weird and scary to me.

✳ December 1, 2008

I have to admit I am feeling lazy and hung over today. Drank too much wine last night! I will have to ask Manuel to get me some coconut water to cure me.

Last night a giant crab almost walked in our bedroom. I found him just walking down the hallway. Honestly, the stupid things that get into your house.

This morning I found another tarantula on the deck by the pool when I took the dogs out. It freaks you out every time! It's a big, hairy, fuzzy, long-legged, nasty looking creature! Yucky! I just tell any big strong man passing by and they have to save me and remove it.

✳ December 2, 2008

Another big fat moon last night and 3 more moonflowers opened up.

This morning there is no rain again! It is sunny and beautiful. I did 2 workouts. It feels good to feel strong. I walked on the beach and found some cool sea glass for my little pile. Really, what makes people collect shit from the beach? I do it and I don't even know why I am collecting it. What will I do with that sea glass? Maybe I can use it like mosaic tile on something. The beach was nice and clean today.

Carly and I went to town on the Mule, which is an open ATV with a bench seat so two people can sit in it. It looks like a golf cart. It rained for maybe 2 minutes just before we got to town and in those 2 minutes we were soaked completely down to our underwear. For one of the two minutes you could barely see because there was so much water in your face. When we got to Rogues we looked like someone had tossed us in a pool with our clothes on. Lucita just laughed at us and fed us some great food. We stayed until we dried out then we went to Casa Alemania which is another restaurant and hotel in town and had a great massage. The owner has a massage studio upstairs and does a really nice job. It was something I never would have done on my own. Carly just decides she wants to do something and we go. After our massages, we went to get some groceries. We attract allot of attention driving this little vehicle. Everyone stops you and asks you how much you paid for it and they all want to look at it. Carly went into the vegetable market and five little boys came around to the vehicle. They were begging me to take them for a ride. They wanted to know my name and where I lived. They were so funny. We stopped in at the Made in Honduras shop and bought some cute baskets. They were made out of pine needles and plastic grocery bags. How creative is that? – made with things people throw out! Even in places where you have no craft supply stores, you cannot stop someone with a creative urge to make something useful or beautiful. Artists will find something available to work with. I like that. Honduras needs more of that creative beautiful spirit.

On the way back to the house, I was noticing that on any road in Trujillo you could be on the road with people walking, a car, truck, pig, horse, dogs, chickens, a donkey, a motorcycle or a Kawasaki Mule.

❄ December 3, 2008

I thought maybe the rainy season was done but nope. It rained all last night and now it is raining hard again this morning. It feels like a big storm is almost upon us. We don't watch the news on local TV like you would in Canada. We rely on other people telling you about what they hear, or you go to a website to show you the tropical storm paths. I guess there is still a bit of rain left in the rainy season.

This morning I found a dead frog on the front porch. Roger said it drowned. I say it got hit in the head like a boulder with that hard rain when it started. All night it rained heavy and steady. It continued all morning until early this afternoon.

I saw Manuel's kids playing in their homemade rain coats. Daniel and Maria were dancing and playing in their black garbage bags with a hole cut out of them for the place you pop your head out of. When it started to rain a bit heavier they lifted their bags to cover their heads. They looked like two little Muslim girls in their burkas walking around. I was totally entertained by them from the kitchen window and they had no idea how funny they were.

I saw four hummingbirds today. This is a rare sight. I don't usually see that many. I think it's because we have some flowers but we don't have allot of red tubular flowers that they like. I have tried to start some Chilean climbing vines a few times but I can't get them to germinate. They would be a fantastic flower to attract the hummingbirds. My moonflowers are doing great. My four o'clocks seem to be finished flowering so I think I will pull them all out and plant some more of the same seeds. They germinate quickly and grow fast.

You have to watch everything when you are here because if someone can steal it they just might. We were at Rogues Galleria and we parked an ATV right in the restaurant with a car parked behind it. We knew the vehicle wasn't going anywhere however, there were some young kids playing near it and they stole the keys. Now I would be the first to say you shouldn't have left the keys in it. I never trust anyone no matter where I live. What would they even want with the keys? Honestly if it's there, remember it's tempting to someone. I hate to think the worst in people but, sometimes this place bums me out so I can't see the good for the bad.

It was such a nice sunny afternoon. Carly and I went to town on the quads and got filthy dirty because of all the muddy roads. We came back and needed to shower but, it was a great time. These roads are a perfect, bumpy track for ATVs.

When we got back there was a cow stuck in the mud just in front of the house in the river. The cows come to graze on the grass on the property and they go to the river to drink water. Since we have had so much rain, when the cow went to get a drink of water in the river she sunk and could not get out. The farmers who own the cows tried to get her out with ropes but could not. It is getting dark now and the guys have left her and will come back in the morning. I am scared for her because of the crocodile in the river. I hope she doesn't die. It is so sad. My heart just aches for the poor beast. Maybe they should have some water in a trough so the cows don't have to go in the river?

I went to see the chubby fat puppies to cheer myself up after being so sad about the cow. They are so cute. There is a black one that is in love with me. I call him Gordo which means fatso in Spanish. Robelio the watchman at the front gate also has a new puppy. They said its mother died. The puppy is so tiny with a big fat distended stomach. I can't believe they all keep getting more dogs. They can't even feed the ones they have.

✳ December 4, 2008

This morning I woke to the sounds of the dogs barking. When I went out, I saw the poor cow sitting on the ground resting after her hard night standing in the river. I don't know how she got out but I saw some cuts on her from the ropes they were trying to use to get her out yesterday. She was just resting and the dogs were running around her barking. She was so tired she didn't give a shit. Normally the dogs scare the cows and help to move them. Not this morning! She was going nowhere until she had a rest first. I tried to figure out how she got out. Manuel said they got her out with the help of a car or a truck. I am so happy she didn't get eaten by the crocodile. I hope she will be alright. I think that if she can walk and eat after she has had a rest maybe she will be ok. A little later some guys from the farm came and lifted her onto the back of a truck on her side and drove her home. I heard from someone else later on that she was ok. Can you imagine guys lifting a full grown cow? This is a time when you would be grateful the cows aren't fat cows like in North America but still it is a full grown cow!

I was making chicken soup for dinner tonight and when I took a container of Italian seasoning and unscrewed the top, somehow a baby gecko fell into my soup. I think he was on the lid and I didn't see him. Thank God it wasn't at a rolling boil. In fact it wasn't really very hot at all. I tried to rescue him when he fell to the bottom and after carefully fishing around with a ladle I found him. I put him on the counter and then I sent him on his way perfectly fine. We ate the soup and didn't care that a gecko fell in it. I boiled it for a bit longer and we survived just fine on Chicken Gecko Soup!

✳ December 5, 2008

I always see things first thing early in the morning when I take out the dogs for a pee. Today I saw two wild green parrots fly by. This is the first time I have seen any parrots of any kind. They stayed in a big tree next door for a few minutes, ate some seeds and then flew away.

It is a nice sunny day. Carly and I did a P90X Kenpo workout and we feel great! We look out the kitchen window this morning while making our breakfast and we notice Manuel's kids playing and running around in the yard. We are completely entertained by their costumes. Daniel and Maria are both wearing black plastic bags like a dress. I am sure they were the same bags they wore as rain coats during the last storm when they looked like two little girls in burkas. It was hilarious to watch them play and entertain themselves for over an hour. They would run and chase each other and then they would fall down and laugh. They would chase little Manuelito and then put him under their dresses and laugh. Back at home, I am sure we would be mortified that they would play with plastic bags. What if they asphyxiate themselves? What if they get caught in it and fall in the water and drown? But in this setting you have to appreciate that the simplest thing can be a toy that entertains and stimulates imagination. They do not have an entire house full of every plastic toy available. They don't sit around saying they are bored. There is something nostalgically pure to be said for this type of play.

These are children who have chores they must do to contribute to helping their family. They work no matter how small. On a sunny afternoon when their chores are done they run and play like little children should everywhere. I wouldn't want this type of hard life for my children but, I also don't think I would want the typical, North American one either. A healthy balance between getting your ass outside and riding your bike or running around playing with your friends to balance with the benefits of computer technology and maybe a little responsibility thrown in might not be so bad. Both are extremes of the other. Maybe a place somewhere in the middle might be just right.

I was thinking of a way I could position Lulu in front of me on the quad without having to hold on to her. I remembered I had a carrying pouch that you strap over your shoulders like a backpack only the pouch is in the front and you can put your dog in it like having her sit in a bag. I could strap it on and then Lulu could sit in the carrier and be contained while I could use both hands on the handle bars. Where is that bag?

Found it! Well, wasn't she just perfectly happy in it? Even after the ride to drop off food she was quite pleased to be carried around in it. I got the impression she was wondering what took me so long to figure this out and could I carry her everywhere, all the time, from now on! Thanks.

The Hondurans wonder where I get this stuff from. Did I actually buy it somewhere and who would have even thought to invent it? I am sure they couldn't imagine half of the stuff we have for dogs much less see the implications for children and carrying them or containing them or entertaining them.

My little Molli is such a sweetheart. I just love her so much. She is old and can't see well but she just happily plods along walking up and down the hallways like a little old lady.

Then she goes back to her pillow for a little nap

We had an evening of high drama.

There are two dogs that are always at the front gate. Tigra and Cheezpa always pal around together. These two dogs always bark and chase the cars as they come in and go past them. Roger has been telling the watchmen forever to train their dogs to stop doing this because it's dangerous.

Today, Jordy one of the men that does work on the property was driving in and the dogs were chasing his truck. He sped up to outrun them and apparently the dogs ran too far in front and he hit them. I heard all of this from Manuel. He said that Jordy killed both of the dogs. He said that those dogs were brothers and that is why they always played together. He told me Robelio is going to kill Jordy because he killed the dogs. Everyone was screaming and very upset. They were not old dogs maybe 9 months to a year old. I am so sad and I understand why dogs just don't live to be old here. It's just all too sad and I am immediately bummed and depressed. Why does this shit always happen here? Peter goes to see Robelio at the front gate and talks him out of killing Jordy. Jordy agrees to get him another dog.

❄ December 6, 2008

I am sitting in the kitchen this morning and all of sudden out of the corner of my eye I see Cheezpa walk by. Yup, one of the dogs that was dead last night just walked by this morning. I go out and look at him. There are no cuts, no bruises, and no indication of any trauma whatsoever. He flips over and lets me rub his belly for a few minutes. This is funny all by itself since up to this point he has never let me even pet his head. Once he has had enough he just walks away.

So......now there is only one dead dog.

This afternoon Carly and I went to go buy some groceries in town. On the way back in, Robelio opens the gate and I look over to my right to look for the fat puppy with the big belly. Out of the corner of my eye I see a dog. I shout "it's Tigra!" Carly says "what?" I say "it's the other dead dog" and we stop the truck. Tigra is lying on the ground and as we walk towards her she wags her tail to greet us. We can see her hip is swollen and she can't get up. I ask Robelio's wife if she is eating and drinking and she says yes. I ask her if she has gone to pee or poop and they say no. The dog allows us to touch her swollen leg. Carly says "I am going to Judy's to see if I can find a vet. We cannot let her suffer." Yeah Carly!

Ten phone calls later we discover there is a guy in Trujillo who may or may not be a vet. His name is Scott and he works with a Cow Mission. (Who even knew there was such a thing?) He can see us right away but if we need to we will have to drive to Tacoa, an hour and a half away, where the closest vet is. Trujillo does not have a vet.

Peter, along with the neighbor's watchman (because he is the only person who knows where Scott lives) and Carly all go with the dog to see Scott in town. When they are trying to load the dog into the truck Robelio who owns the dog picks her up roughly and she almost bites him. When they get to Scott's, Peter gently lifts her out of the truck and she is fine. Scott says she has a broken femur and it would take pins and extensive surgery to possibly help fix the leg. They could only do this surgery 5 hours away in San Pedro. Hell, the bumpy car ride would probably kill the poor dog. He said she doesn't seem to be crying out in pain or suffering and he cannot see any indications of internal bleeding or other injuries. He said let her rest a few weeks and she will probably be fine. The leg will be lame but, she will be fine and she will learn to manage. So they take Tigra back home. I found an old sleeping bag so she can lie on something softer than concrete. I am just so happy they don't shoot her and steal the sleeping bag. So at the end of the day there are no dead dogs. That's good. Honestly, why do they make shit up? Note to self, if someone says the dog is dead, ask to see the dog.

When they get back from the vet we notice that Manuel has tied up his dogs so they don't chase the cars. He doesn't want his dogs to be hit by a car and there are so many cars that come and go around here. I understand why they chase things. If an animal tries to come from the beach they bark and chase it. If the cows get too close to the house, the dogs help to move them back by barking and chasing. And a car is just another kind of intruder. I hope they teach them not to chase the cars. Manuel shows that he cares and is doing the best he can. I am so bummed by the whole affair. I don't want to care and I am mad at myself because I do.

✳ December 7, 2008

Manuel is going to have eye surgery. He has some non-cancerous growths on both his eyes. It is similar to a cataract in that it eventually covers the eye, causes headaches and can cause blindness. This condition is common in tropical places when people do not wear sunglasses. Roger is going to pay the 4800 lempira per eye (which is around $250 dollars) to help Manuel. It is a quick laser procedure done in La Ceiba. Manuel cannot get to La Ceiba because he doesn't have a car and cannot pay for the procedure or the medicine. Roger will arrange for his transportation and make sure he gets what he needs. This is a very generous gift from Roger and Manuel knows it.

There are many eye clinics in Honduras and lots of eye troubles. The tropical sun is a very powerful thing and does much damage. Doctors come several times a year from all over the world to volunteer their time and go from town to town providing help to those who cannot come to the larger cites.

We went to see Tigra today and she was resting quietly. Her swelling had gone down about 50% from yesterday. She didn't feel like eating or drinking but she let us touch her leg and she was wagging her tail. I hope she will be ok.

The guys who do all the refinishing of doors and windows are here today. They used to hate me and now for some reason they seem to like me. They take so long to finish everything. Every door is done by hand. It usually takes weeks to finish sanding and only one person is allowed to spray on the varnish. Do not get me wrong they are beautiful when they are done but, what happened is they underestimated the job and now they have run out of money. So now after 3 months they are hurrying to finish and so the pool side of the house is not as nicely done as the front. Mahogany is really a beautiful wood and even though the weather is so harsh it is one of the only woods that can withstand the weather, the ants and the termites. It is beautiful but wood requires maintenance.

This evening there were a million fruit flies in the kitchen for some reason. I looked up a homemade remedy and found if you put cider vinegar in a bowl with some dish soap they will be attracted and then get trapped in the soap and drown. It is amazing to see how many we can catch with this simple remedy. The internet is a beautiful thing.

✳ December 8, 2008

I am tired today. I am sad and weary. I am ready to go home. I am tired because it's raining and the rain reminds me how I feel. I am so tired of being bitten by mosquitoes all the time no matter what I do or don't do. No matter what I spray, if I wear long pants or not they still bite me. I try to see the good and the beautiful but, the ugly or the hard usually shines through. It is a hard place to get to know. There are unusual ways and customs. I just think I do not have that kind of day in day out fight and willingness to play their game to survive. If you want to live in the wild west, this is it. If you think that rustic is your way, then this is it. If you think living in a cost effective place on the beach is the most important thing, then this is it. If you want to carve your own way, then you will love it. Many people do.

I find it just beats me down and it is so hard to be here alone most of the time. Peter and I just don't have enough of an edge to fit in and be respected. I don't understand or want to play this game. It's just too hard to learn the rules and I feel like I can never, ever win.

Hunger: noun

A feeling of discomfort or weakness caused by lack of food.

Verb: have a strong desire or craving for

Synonyms: starvation-famine-longing-yearning-craving

I have dreams of grocery stores with organic sections and paved roads and air conditioning. I want to go home, to feel like myself again. I have such dark thoughts and I can go there in a second from something stupid that happens. I can't be in a place where life is not valued and kindness not accepted without scepticism. I can't figure out the rules. I find I am losing myself and I cover my personality with layer and layer of quietness to protect what I have left of me. I want to believe I just can't see.

Tigra was up and walking around. It looked like she almost was putting weight on her back leg. There is still some swelling but, she is looking much better.

Tigra feeling much better

※ December 9, 2008

I went to Miami for a few days this past weekend. I bought some flea and tick medication for the watchmen's dogs. It was just the cheap kind you can buy in any pet store. As soon as I came back I went to put it on the dogs and once again the watchmen and their families were fascinated by what I was doing. They had never seen a medicine to prevent fleas and ticks and were surprised I would get this for their dogs. I also bought all the dogs a nice collar. I missed my little dogs and was so happy to hug them and kiss them both. I was happy to see my husband Peter most of all.

Manuel went for his eye surgery. The following day he had to go into the clinic in town for a check-up. They gave him some eye drops and told him to put them in his eyes every 4 hours. The drops had to be kept in the fridge so we had to keep them in our house. Carly went over to his house each time he needed his drops. She is the nurse for the people around here and I am the nurse for the animals. I wonder if they even have a clock? They must. It is like having dependent adults living on your property. They can just barely manage their daily lives and if there is any kind of maintenance or something out of the normal they just don't know how to cope. It snaps me back to reality when I consider how rich we are and how fortunate we are simply by being born in the developed world. We simply take our fortunes for granted. I look at my dogs and our lives. We are all so spoiled. My dogs sleep on clean pillows and blankets and eat organic food. I am thankful for all I have and grateful for the country I grew up in and grateful to my parents for making the difficult journey to leave communist Czechoslovakia and find their way to Canada for a better life.

Tigra is running up to greet me this morning and she is happy to say hello and almost back to her old self.

✳ December 10, 2008

Peter and I have colds or the flu today and we both feel like shit.

When I dropped off the dog food tonight Manuel's wife and his kids were very anxious to show me that their two puppies got attacked by the crocodile last night. They both escaped but the blonde puppy has a big cut on her ear and my pal Gordo, the black puppy, somehow got his leg hurt. He was all quiet and won't get up to meet me. I move his leg and it looks sore but I don't think it's broken. I went back to the house and got some tee tree oil and some antiseptic ointment and I cleaned the puppy's ear and wiped it with tee tree oil. Gordo will not get up. I wrapped him up in a little blanket and pet him for a few minutes while they tell me all the awful details.

✳ December 11, 2008

There was a fiesta today at the foot of the first housing development. It was to celebrate all the roads going in. There was supposed to be a party at the top of the mountain but there has been too much rain. It even rained all of today right up to the beginning of the party. Everyone was so relieved when it finally stopped. There was food and dancing and fireworks. People came from Canada and all parts of Honduras. There were people all dressed up looking their best and it was a nice opportunity to get together and celebrate this milestone. At one point Carly asked Roger if he was going to make a speech but, he had to wait until the translator got back. The translator was helping get the bus out of the ditch. We laughed because that's what happens here and in the end it all turned out perfectly. The generator finally got the lights working and the food and entertainment were lovely. A fiesta is always a good time.

✳ December 12, 2008

Today I saw a beautiful rainbow, not just a fragment but a whole rainbow. I think it is a sign of hope and rebirth.

We have decided to go home. If a place cannot bring out the best in you, then perhaps it is a sign that something is not right. I have tried to pull out every resourceful, creative part of me in order to function and provide service and find a way to learn and grow but, I find it eats me rather than nourishes and builds on the small parts I do enjoy. I shut down from the realities and constant uphill battles rather than let them fuel me to prove I can do this. In all other times in my life when I was faced with something that someone said I could not do I was compelled to prove them wrong but, I feel this place has beat this out of me and I have given up. I have tried with every tool I have to motivate and inspire and force myself to go through this difficult period in order to come through on the other side to see the fruits of all the hard work and face the progress that will inevitably come. I know there will be much positive growth for this area. There will be new tourism and more jobs for the people that live here. It's just a matter of time. I am sorry to give up but, I am ready to leave.

I planted 10 papaya saplings all along the fence between the property and the neighbor's fence. I started some seeds from a beautiful tree that looks like an orchid – the locals call it Pata de Vaca or "footprint of a cow" because the leaves look like a cow's footprint. I also planted a coconut. I am sorry I will not see them mature. Maybe I will come back again someday as a visitor to see what has happened.

My small orchid tree

This is the Orchid tree (Bauhinia) or the cows' footprint as the locals call it (Pata de Vaca). It has the most beautiful orchid like flowers.

The little kids are all running around today with frozen Kool-Aid that they are eating from a little clear bag. It is just like we used to do when we were kids. In Canada there was a long frozen stick called a Mr. Freeze. The next door neighbor's watchman has a fridge in his little house. This is quite a big deal and all the other watchmen use his fridge for some of their things. Someone buys the powder and makes the Kool-Aid and pours it into plastic bags and then they just eat it when it's frozen. People are more the same than they are different in all places. Children should all be happy enjoying a sunny day with a frozen treat.

You hear crazy things happening every day. The heat makes people nuts sometimes. Today we heard a man went to a disco in town and found his wife and beat her until he thought she was dead. Then he was so distraught he killed their kids. Oh my God!

Then another man thought some guy was fooling around with his wife so he shot him right in the middle of the town square. This is nothing new. Bad things happen in every part of the world every day. For some reason it just seems too close to me.

We went to the bank in Trujillo to get a certified cheque for our shipping container and they said they can't do certified cheques, they don't have the machine...honestly.

The roads suck. Sometimes they are better than other times. They are dirt roads and they get giant pot holes in them. They fix them and then it rains and they get really bad again. You normally need to drive pretty cautiously and sometimes very slowly because it wrecks your vehicle. You must never, ever travel without a spare tire because you will get a flat. It's just a matter of when. There are people with bad backs that will not even go into town at all because they get bounced around too much.

❋ December 13, 2008

We have been making plans to get our container on a boat to get back to Canada. Do you know how suspect you are when you are leaving Honduras after 6 months with personal belongings? Most companies may allow you to ship personal belongings from another country into Honduras but very few will touch personal shipments leaving. It is such a gateway for illegal drug trafficking and they want nothing to do with it so most will only do business shipments. Finally we make arrangements from the connections we made in Canada getting our stuff here. We have arranged to hire a flatbed truck to get the container from the house to the Port of Castilla. Then it will get on a Dole ship to Delaware and from Delaware it will travel by truck to Vancouver. We have decided to move to Vancouver since Peter always wanted to move there and the 2010 Olympics are coming. He would like to be doing something that is working on the Olympics. Before we left for Honduras this was a consideration and we chose Honduras. Now that we have decided to leave early this is a way we get to try both.

We gave away lots of the boxes we unpacked and now we had to go get them back because you cannot buy boxes in town or even in La Ceiba. I guess there is no market for boxes. The only boxes you can get are small boxes that some food comes in from grocery stores. Imagine no boxes to move!

❋ December 14, 2008

The flatbed arrived today. We surprised ourselves and have made all the arrangements in crazy fast time. Everything takes so much time to make anything happen and this is truly amazing that everything just fell perfectly into place to make it all happen quickly.

We have 4 days from Monday through Thursday to pack all the stuff up into the container and be at the port. It sounds like a lot of time right? WRONG. We didn't unpack all of our belongings from the container, however we must pack all the things we have in the bedroom and kitchen and a few outside things like chairs and some lawn equipment. Then we also need to take out every single thing that is currently in the container so they can lift it on to the flatbed when it is empty.

Then we must re-pack the whole thing to fit perfectly tightly to travel over the sea bouncing journey in four days.

Moving the container to the truck

✳ December 17, 2008

So it's done. We have re-loaded the container with the help of many guys. Peter has gone to the Port of Castilla to see if we can get our container on the Dole Ship that is leaving December 23. We also have our trip to Vancouver booked for the same day. We have to make sure the container goes and then get going ourselves.

We also have to go to the vet's in La Ceiba to get them to sign documents that allow us to take our dogs out... It's just another piece of red tape and someone else to pay.

I cleaned up after everyone left the house and I made something to eat. I feel so much better, sitting in the kitchen. The house is clean and back in original order. I am hopeful that we will be able to get the container on the ship. I hope it won't cost too much to get it out. A few more days and we will be leaving.

Manuel's puppies are getting big now. My pal, the little black one that I was calling Gordo, has been officially named Bonita. I always thought she was a boy!

Look how cute the puppies are with their collars. Lulu wants nothing to do with any of them. She is such a snob. She never likes any other dogs. They have both recovered from their crocodile attack and both the ear and the leg are fine.

❋ December 18, 2008

Peter drove Manuel to La Ceiba today for an eye appointment. He phones me to tell me that he is stuck in traffic in Tacoa. He told me they got out to see what the problem was. There at the front of the line is a truck with a guy on the ground beside it DEAD! Blood is pouring out of his head. Later we heard two stories: one, that he just fell off the back of the truck and he cracked his head and two, that someone killed him off the back of the truck! Who knows? I know how bumpy the roads are and if you just sit on the ledge of the bed of the truck it is so easy to imagine someone falling off.

So Peter went to the bank in La Ceiba to get a certified cheque, since we could not get one in Trujillo. He goes to the teller to withdraw the balance and they give him the money plus the certified cheque. He asks them 3 times if the amount they are giving him back is correct. And they say yes.

Then on the drive back the bank calls him to say you can't cash that cheque because there is no money in your account. Ridiculous! So on the way home he goes to another bank to deposit the value of the check back into the account.

Clearly they don't have a clue what a certified cheque is and that they need to take the money out of your account and allow the check to be cashed!

The cleaning lady Magdalena came this morning. She brought two of her sons with her. One son is 10 years old and the other is 12. They are both drinking her coffee. I don't remember kids drinking coffee when I was that age. What child would even like the taste? Hell I didn't start drinking coffee until I was 21 and had to work an overnight shift. Magdalena says that her oldest kid is going to college next year. They call high school college. I spoke to them about school and she said the average kid goes to school until they are about 10 years old. Normally it's only half days because there are too many kids and not enough classrooms and schools. This way they share the classrooms. But if you calculate it out most of them get about 4 years education as we know it and many don't even go consistently. When it is the rainy season, most don't go so the rainy season is like the North American summer break. They are off from October through December and then they start again after Christmas. Everyone tells you something different about school and education.

It's quite strange that lately I have noticed that I have not been using too much bug spray. For some reason the bugs are not bothering me that much. Is this the turning point for me when I become less tasty to the mosquitoes? Seriously, how can this be happening the minute before we are leaving? We still get attacked at night when we sleep but I can walk to the front gate in the evening just before dark and I am not bothered lately. Maybe it's something as simple as there are fewer mosquitoes now that it is cooler? Who cares? I am glad!

❄ December 19, 2008

Today is a beautiful Saturday morning and our last in Honduras. Today the Honduran sun is perfect, the breeze is light and the sky is blue. Honduras is laughing at us for leaving because today it is paradise!

Our last Saturday in Honduras

I am not looking forward to the journey with the dogs in their traveling cases but I am excited about getting back to Canada and spending Christmas there. I can't wait to get to the grocery store and see what I can buy. I am going back to the "old country" as my Dad would say!

❄ December 20, 2008

A bird flew into the house today and just as quickly flew out! I decided that it was a good luck omen for the journey home. I went into the bedroom and there was another bird in there! Wow – two in one day!

❄ December 21, 2008

It's our last day in the house. Tomorrow we drive 5 hours to San Pedro Sula, and stay in a hotel overnight. The following day we travel to Houston and then to Vancouver. We get in at midnight on the morning of Christmas Eve. Just enough time to go shopping for Christmas! We have rented a furnished apartment for a month downtown and from there we will have to figure out what to do. Where to live, buy a car and so on.

And so the sun sets on this chapter of the adventure and off to the next one. There will always be tomorrow to look forward to!

✳ December 22, 2008

On the way to San Pedro I saw how they fill up dump trucks. By hand with shovels! Wow this place still has the ability to amaze me.

I saw a guy driving a motorcycle with a baby in between his legs. Neither one had a helmet on!

Now it just sounds like a comedy routine.

So the 5 hour drive to San Pedro Sula was good if not extremely bumpy. The drive is good for preparing the dogs for the airplane journey. We had to sneak Molli and Lulu into the hotel because there is no such thing as a dog friendly hotel here. We got a room on the second floor but it was right near an exit door so we could just take them in their carriers. No one would even dream that a dog was in those gym bags. We put down some pee pads in the room. The dogs didn't get to go out for a pee from 6 pm to 9 am the next morning. That is a very long time for them but, they did all their business before we got on the plane and they were great until we got to Houston.

We were able to leave the top flaps open on the dog carry cases and they seemed to be fine as long as they saw us. That way we could talk to them and pet them and they would just go back to sleep. We finally arrived in Vancouver at 1 am. When we took the dogs outside to pee there was snow on the ground. They hadn't seen snow in a long time and Molli really didn't like the cold. We finally got our stuff, got into our taxi and made our way to the apartment.

✳ December 24, 2008

The key was left for us under a flower pot. When we all ploughed into bed at 2:30 am with the covers all up nice and toasty we were exhausted. It snowed all night long and all the following day but, it was Christmas Eve! And snow is perfect on Christmas Eve!

We were so happy that we made the long trip with only one lost piece of luggage that would follow after. I was so excited to go to the grocery store. I was giddy when I saw all my choices for Christmas dinner. I was so excited to see all the fresh vegetables I could buy. It was better than being in a candy shop. This was the most snow that Vancouver had since 1964 and we discovered that ours was one of the last flights to land before the airport was closed this morning. It was all just perfect.

We saw 2 hummingbirds outside our window which is odd since I have never seen hummingbirds in the snow before! I am sure this is a good omen!

I made a delicious roasted turkey breast dinner with all the trimmings for a wonderful Christmas feast. The dogs were fine and we were happy to start again in a new place. It was a postcard Christmas with my perfect family.

Nourish: verb

Provide with substances necessary for growth, health and good condition.

To keep alive. To maintain.

Everyplace has its pros and cons. There are times when you feel the grass is greener someplace else. Life is about where you are at this very moment in time and what is important to you now.

Every place has taxes to be paid and it isn't always paid to the government. What I have learned is you always pay in some way. You just need to determine what taxes you are willing to pay and which you are not.

Many people love Honduras. You can buy beachfront property for a fraction of the cost of other vacation places in the world. You can build a beautiful home at an amazing price. The taxes are low, the cost of living is good, food is inexpensive and cocktail hour is cheap. There are many benefits to encourage foreigners to invest in the country. Health care is good and inexpensive. I recently heard of a man from British Columbia who went to Honduras from Canada to get some extensive dental work done at a fraction of the cost in Canada. Labour is inexpensive, so you can hire people to help you as well as providing much appreciated local employment.

For most the pull is avoiding the cold winters and living someplace new and exciting.

Since we were there in 2008 so many improvements and developments have increased the desirability of Honduras and Trujillo in particular. I am optimistic for the future of the country and excited about the little town I lived in briefly.

Sometimes it takes a long time to look back and see the lessons learned and to give thanks. I was not able to see clearly for almost four years after.

Honduras was a journey into the unknown. It was a gift because it showed me that we could take a big leap and JUMP! I am thankful for many heart opening moments and thankful to have felt the sadness and pain that comes with self discovery and internal growth. It is the challenging moments in life that teach you the biggest lessons. I learned that I need to be open to new experiences and places. Being open helps you to accept more, to learn more and to love more. I learned for the first time in my life that if I am not passionate and fuelled by something, it is not for me, no matter how hard I try to fake it.

It is at the core of me, not right!

Each experience is a teacher. The question is: are you paying attention to the teacher? I was sad and lonely even when there were a thousand people around me. Sometimes you need to leave to make room for someone else to discover their place in our role. Maybe it was their time to be there and not mine. I learned that if it doesn't feel natural at some level it won't work.

I will only listen to the voice in my own head to be the guide for me. In the worst times of my life I am not the person that can just talk it through with friends or family. I simply need to close out the noise of the world and go within for answers. I want to be sure that the decisions I make are mine alone and not influenced by others. True heartache has to be solved in my own soul.

I have discovered I am moved by beauty in the simplest things and moments. Perhaps the artist in me is moved by that in the world. An animal can open me up like a can of sardines. Flowers and nature can bring me to tears and initiate a desire to create. Food can be a canvas to create a masterpieces as well as nourishment.

I felt surrounded by sadness, fear, depression and anger. Like in Harry Potter when Ron is in the presence of a *dementor* and says "it was as if I would never feel cheered again". I could not and would not see the potential, just the overwhelming impossible battle. Without the joyful discovery of it all, I felt smaller and smaller until I was paralysed. I wanted to run away. I prayed to get out!

I know leaving was the right thing for me. I am grateful to be where I am for many reasons.

Almost 4 years later I am ready and truly excited to go back for a visit.

As I write this I stare down at the glass of wine in my hand. I think of glass again. This time I see the beauty of the clear crystal and the deep red of the rich Shiraz within. I bring it to my lips and savour the smell and taste. I raise my glass to celebrate the combination of grapes, earth, warmth and time. I breathe deeply and smile as I realize that I am like the glass: clear and strong and far better able to show the contents within. I am better for this experience and richer for my short time in Trujillo.

If the only prayer you ever say in your entire life is thank you, it will be enough.

Meister Eckhart

Epilogue

I travelled back for a short visit in August 2012 and I was absolutely and completely dazzled and amazed by everything that has been accomplished by the many dedicated people who have believed in the vision and had the fortitude and tenacity to make it happen.

There are beautiful vacation homes built and a fantastic park system complete with a world class zoo showcasing and rehabilitating rescued animals local to the country. The cruise ship terminal is currently under construction and ships are already scheduled for 2013. There are new restaurants and attractions to interest and excite tourism in the area. They have all done an awesome and truly amazing job.

I was honoured and excited to see everything that has been created and the progress made. I am sure I will be back for another visit and I encourage you to go explore Trujillo if your travels take you there.

Much Love
Hilda

CPSIA information can be obtained at www.ICGtesting.com
Printed in the USA
LVOW052038060613

337360LV00001B/38/P